Stoic
Philosophy
for Beginners

Simple Strategies to Build an Unbreakable
Core, Withstand Life's Toughest Tests,
Discover the Power of Pausing Before You
Act, and Achieve Lasting Well-Being

CalmLogic Press

CONTENTS

Applying Stoic Wisdom

Conclusion

ACKNOWLEDGEMENTS

I would like to extend my heartfelt thanks to all the advanced readers who took the time to delve into the early drafts of this book. Your insightful feedback and invaluable suggestions have been instrumental in refining this narrative and enriching its depth. Your engagement and thoughtful critiques have not only enhanced this work but also inspired and encouraged me throughout this journey. I am immensely grateful for your contributions and for the pivotal role you have played in bringing this book to life. Thank you for your support.

"...excellent primer for those of us just beginning our serious exploration of Stoicism." -R. Leiken

"(It) really does wonders for simplifying and explaining Stoicism and its origins. I would recommend it over (Meditations) or Epictetus and Seneca's writings for an introduction. I think it's more immediately applicable." – R. Cowles

BONUS DOWNLOAD

FREE DAILY STOICISM JOURNAL

Stoic Philosophy for Beginners is your accessible guide to adopting Stoic practices that foster resilience, thoughtful decision-making, and deep contentment. This book simplifies the profound teachings of Stoicism into practical steps that you can apply to your life right away, helping you to control what you can and accept what you cannot.

To further aid your exploration of Stoic principles, we have crafted the **Daily Stoicism Journal**. This 21-day journal complements the strategies discussed in the book with daily quotes, meditations, and exercises, deepening your understanding and application of Stoicism each day.

Download your free copy of the **Daily Stoicism Journal** to begin your practical journey into Stoicism and experience its transformative effects. Scan the QR code with your phone to start your download:

Embrace this opportunity to enhance your resilience and find lasting well-being through the wisdom of Stoicism.

INTRODUCTION

Life is long if you know how to use it. –Seneca

The above statement challenges our perception of life itself. In an era where we often hear about the scarcity of time, Seneca's profound wisdom serves as a reminder that it is abundant if we use it wisely.

Stoicism, an ancient Greek philosophy, offers much more than just a set of beliefs: It also provides practical tools for personal growth and resilience. As we navigate the complexities of modern life, the principles of virtue, mindfulness, and emotional resilience are more relevant than ever. By integrating these practices into our daily routines, we can transform our lives, making significant strides in our journey toward self-improvement.

Stoic Philosophy for Beginners: Simple Strategies to Build an Unbreakable Core, Withstand Life's Toughest Tests, Discover the Power of Pausing Before You Act, and Achieve Lasting Well-Being therefore aims to reveal the secrets of this ancient system of beliefs, demonstrating how its timeless principles can solve modern problems and guide you to become your best self.

In this book, you will discover how to apply ancient wisdom to overcome the challenges you currently face. Whether it's dealing with stress, finding purpose, or building resilience, Stoicism offers a path to a more fulfilling life. We will explore the powerful impact of daily routines on personal growth, emphasizing how as little as 10 to 15 minutes a day can lead to profound changes.

We will also delve into the essence of this ancient practice, not through repeating abstract theory but by presenting a hands-on guide for day-to-day living. This book is crafted to serve not just as a repository of knowledge but as a practical manual for initiating tangible change in your life. Each chapter will unpack ancient teachings in a way that is directly applicable to modern challenges, emphasizing that even a few minutes of deliberate, daily philosophical practice can help you yield significant strides toward personal enlightenment and growth.

By distilling the wisdom of Stoic philosophy into actionable insights, we aim to equip you with the means to effortlessly adjust your mindset, aligning it more closely with your vision of an ideal self and an enriched life. Beyond the theoretical exploration it presents, this book stands as a call to action—inviting you to implement small yet powerful changes in your perspective and behavior. These shifts are grounded in centuries-old wisdom, but they have been tailored for today's fast-paced world.

With a focus on accessibility, we will navigate the profound depths of Stoic thought, translating it into practical strategies for fostering resilience, purpose, and contentment. Whether you're seeking solace from the stress of daily commitments or aspiring toward a more meaningful existence, this guide offers a clear path forward. Its purpose is to make philosophy work for you, to guide you in turning Stoic concepts into a living practice that moves you, step by step, toward a life of greater fulfillment and tranquility.

This book aims to paint a vivid picture of a better life, one where you are in control of your emotions, aligned with your values, and living each day with purpose and tranquility.

As the author, I bring not only a deep understanding of Stoic philosophy but also practical experience in applying its principles to everyday life. This book synthesizes ancient wisdom with modern insights, offering a fresh perspective on how to navigate challenges with grace and resilience.

You will find more than just information here. You will also find a path to transformation. If you are ready to embark on a journey of self-discovery and personal growth, join me. Together, we will explore how this ancient system of beliefs can unlock your full potential and help you lead a more meaningful and fulfilling life.

CHAPTER ONE

STOICISM 101: THE FUNDAMENTALS OF AN ANCIENT WISDOM

You are living as if destined to live forever; your own frailty never occurs to you; you don't notice how much time has already passed, but squander it as though you had a full and overflowing supply—though all the while that very day which you are devoting to somebody or something may be your last. You act like mortals in all that you fear and like immortals in all that you desire. (Maden, 2021) -Seneca

Have you been living with the mindset that you will live forever? Upon reflecting on Seneca's words, it becomes clear that the initial and most crucial realization we must embrace is acknowledging that time is not an infinite resource.

In the quoted passage, the ancient Stoic is highlighting the contradiction in human behavior, where we fear death yet live as if we will never die, neglecting our mortality and the swift passage of time. He urges us to recognize life's brevity and to prioritize meaningful pursuits over trivial ones. The core message emphasizes the importance of living each day fully and purposefully (Alaili, 2022).

Many of us unknowingly live as though we will always be here. We carry on as if we are immune to the passage of time, rarely acknowledging our vulnerability. We fail to grasp how much of our lives has already slipped away, treating the prospect of a new day as an abundant and never-ending commodity.

It is in this unawareness that we waste the very hours and moments that could potentially be our last. However, by accepting the finite nature of our existence and heeding the wisdom contained within the pages of this book, you will take your first step toward personal growth, experiencing a profound shift in your perspective and approach to life.

What Is Philosophy?

At the heart of philosophical inquiry is the pursuit of wisdom. This is not just academic but deeply practical, influencing how we make decisions, how we relate to others, and how we navigate the complexities of life. "Philosophy," derived from the Greek words "philo" (love) and "Sophia" (wisdom), literally means the love of wisdom. This encapsulates its fundamental aim to seek and embody the search for understanding in all aspects of life.

Philosophy, at its core, is a quest for understanding—it is the exploration of fundamental truths about ourselves, the world around us, and our place within it. It delves into questions of existence, knowledge, values, reason, the mind, and language through critical, systematic approaches and rational argumentation.

The pursuit of wisdom teaches us to think critically, argue effectively, and live thoughtfully. It is both a discipline and a way of life, offering frameworks for understanding the world and guiding principles for ethical living. It encourages us to examine our beliefs, challenge our assumptions, and seek deeper insights into the nature of reality and our experiences.

Philosophy encompasses a vast range of subdisciplines, each providing unique perspectives on questions that have intrigued humans for centuries.

- **Metaphysics:** What is the nature of reality?

- **Epistemology:** Can we truly know anything?

- **Ethics:** What is the right thing to do?

- **Logic:** How should we reason?

- **Aesthetics:** What is beauty?

- **Political philosophy:** What is the best form of government?

Through the lens of philosophy, we learn to appreciate the complexity of these questions and the diversity of possible answers. Philosophers, from ancient times to the modern era—ranging from Socrates, Plato, and Aristotle to Descartes, Kant, and beyond—have left us with rich legacies of thought and debate. Their ideas challenge us to think deeply, question persistently, and live more reflectively.

The discipline's relevance extends beyond abstract theorizing to impact real-world issues. It equips us with the tools to tackle ethical dilemmas, navigate moral complexities, and engage in meaningful discussions about the challenges society is facing. In this way, philosophy is not just about contemplating life's big questions but about applying wisdom to make a difference in the world.

Ethics

Now that we have introduced philosophy and its subdisciplines, we can assess that Stoicism finds its home within the realm of ethics, one of the most applied and personally relevant fields of philosophical inquiry.

Ethics, or moral philosophy, investigates the concepts of right and wrong behavior, moral responsibility, and the foundations of principled living. Its inquiries delve into the nature of justice, rights, virtue, and what is good, seeking to articulate and defend the principles that should guide individual and collective behavior. It poses questions such as:

- What is the good life?

- What duties do we owe to others?

- What constitutes moral virtue?

Stoicism, with its emphasis on virtue, reason, and self-control, offers a distinctive ethical stance. It teaches that the key to a good and fulfilling life lies not in external possessions or social status but in living in accordance with virtue and reason. Stoics believe that by focusing on our individual behavior and attitudes, we can achieve tranquility and satisfaction, regardless of external circumstances. This perspective is deeply ethical, as it places the responsibility for moral conduct and personal well-being squarely on our shoulders, advocating for a life led by principles rather than by the pursuit of pleasure or the avoidance of pain.

The ethical questions Stoicism addresses are not just ancient curiosities. They are deeply relevant to our modern lives. In a world where external success is often valued above character, this belief system reminds us of the importance of values such as integrity, courage, and justice. The challenges of living ethically in a complex, interconnected world—navigating dilemmas in personal relationships, professional life, and global citizenship—echo the Stoic concern with living a virtuous life amid uncontrollable external forces. Therefore, it provides a timeless ethical framework that encourages reflection on what it means to live well, emphasizing personal responsibility, resilience, and the pursuit of integrity in everyday life.

What Is Stoicism?

Stoicism is a philosophical belief system that emphasizes living in harmony with nature and asserts that true happiness is derived from within, not from external circumstances. It advocates for self-control and resilience to overcome harmful emotions, promoting a virtuous life grounded in reason. The philosophy has been enriched by notable thinkers like Seneca, Epictetus, and Marcus Aurelius, who underscored the importance of inner peace and ethical principles over material wealth and success.

Origins and History of Stoicism

Stoicism originated around the 3rd century B.C.E. in Cyprus with Zeno of Citium. It gained prominence during the Hellenistic period and the Roman era, significantly influencing Western thought. The term "Stoic" comes from the Greek word "Stoa," which means porch—this is because this is where Zeno used to teach his students from (Weaver, 2019).

The philosophy, drawing on Socratic teachings, was shaped by the Cynics and the Megarians, who emphasized simplicity and logical rigor. It is known for its practical approach, and it divides philosophy into logic, physics, and ethics. Its enduring appeal lies in its advocacy for inner strength, rationality, and tranquility in the face of life's challenges.

Modern Resurgence: Stoicism and Cognitive Behavioral Therapy

Stoicism isn't limited to only helping us through tough times; it has practical applications in our daily lives as well. It equips us with tools to make wiser decisions, enhance our relationships, and cultivate contentment. It encourages self-reflection and personal development, enabling us to grasp the ever-changing nature of life. It reminds us that this mindset is relevant not only during hardships but also in good times, too.

The ongoing popularity of Stoicism in today's self-help books shows its lasting value and its similarity to the fundamental principles of cognitive behavioral therapy (CBT), offering a way of thinking that helps people better manage their emotions and think more logically.

CBT has its roots in Stoicism. The connection between the two has been highlighted since the 1950s when psychoanalysts rediscovered the ancient philosophy (Robertson, 2022). As one example, the teaching of Epictetus that our reactions are shaped not by events but by our thoughts about them plays a key role in CBT. This concept teaches that how we think and believe affects how we feel, which is central to this mode of therapy.

Acknowledging the link between Stoicism and CBT offers us a deep understanding of psychology: We control our feelings and mental state not by changing what happens around us but by changing how we view it. This idea is at the heart of CBT techniques, which help people spot and change negative or unhelpful thoughts, leading to better feelings and actions. For example, the Stoic method of questioning our initial reactions to see if they match reality is similar to CBT's approach to fixing wrong or harmful thoughts. Both disciplines also agree on the importance of confronting fears and discomfort to foster growth. In CBT, this is known as exposure therapy.

This shared emphasis on self-awareness, logical thinking, and actively improving our thought patterns shows Stoicism's lasting influence on modern therapy. It therefore provides strategies for resilience, happiness, and a stronger approach to handling life's hurdles.

Is It About Being "Stoic"?

Many people confuse the terms "Stoic" and "stoic" and therefore misunderstand the former, which refers to the philosophical school. Meanwhile, the latter denotes emotional restraint or indifference (Atlas, 2021).

Common misconceptions have developed from this. One is that Stoicism promotes suppressing our emotions and being detached. In reality, it teaches us how to manage our feelings and cultivate inner tranquility through rationality. Another common misconception is that it encourages passivity and conformity. On the contrary, it emphasizes active virtue and taking personal responsibility. The belief system promotes a strong, rational, and emotionally intelligent approach to dealing with life's challenges.

Furthermore, it is important to clarify that Stoicism is not synonymous with being unfeeling or indifferent to the joys and sorrows of life (Barbosa, 2020). This misconception often arises because the philosophy emphasizes not being controlled by emotions. Instead of apathy, Stoicism teaches the importance of responding to life's fluctuations with serenity and rationality. By following these principles, we can learn to stay calm and handle whatever comes our way. So, it's not about feeling nothing but about dealing with life in a sensible way.

The Four Cardinal Virtues

Stoic philosophy revolves around the classification of virtue into four main types: wisdom, justice, courage, and temperance. These are not mere ideals but practical guidelines for leading a fulfilling and ethical life. They require us to engage in self-reflection, make ethical decisions, display resilience in the face of adversity, and exercise restraint in our actions and desires (Lake, 2022).

Within Stoicism, embodying the virtues means recognizing that virtue alone is the ultimate good and everything else is inconsequential (Ursulean, 2022). This perspective aids us in concentrating on what truly matters, leading to a life of contentment and tranquility. Practicing wisdom, justice, courage, and temperance serves not only personal growth but also allows us to make a positive impact on society.

Wisdom

Wisdom refers to understanding what is morally right and wrong, which helps in making rational and ethical choices. It is developed by continuously learning and making thoughtful decisions.

Wisdom Challenged

Imagine a person navigating a complex family dispute, where emotions run high, and each party believes they are in the right. The challenge to wisdom arises in understanding the deeper issues at play, recognizing the emotions and perspectives of each family member, and guiding the conversation toward a resolution that acknowledges and respects everyone's feelings and needs. Wisdom in this context means moving beyond our own perspective, employing empathy and rational thought to mediate the dispute and foster harmony within the family.

Justice

Justice involves treating others fairly, showing kindness, and taking responsibility for our actions within society. It is applied by treating others with fairness and compassion, which fosters a sense of community and social responsibility.

Justice Challenged

Consider a scenario where a friend confides in you about having committed a minor wrongdoing, such as taking credit for someone else's work in a community project. The challenge to justice here involves balancing loyalty to your friend with the ethical obligation to ensure fairness and accountability. Acting justly might mean encouraging your friend to correct the mistake by acknowledging the true contributor's work, thus upholding the principles of fairness and integrity in personal relationships and community engagements.

Courage

Courage in Stoicism extends beyond physical bravery to include the ability to face difficulties and ethical dilemmas with strength. It is built by facing our fears and ethical challenges with moral strength.

Courage Challenged

You may witness a friend or family member engaging in self-destructive behavior, such as substance abuse or engaging in toxic relationships. The challenge to courage lies in confronting the person about their behavior despite your concerns about damaging the relationship. True courage is shown by facing these fears and addressing the issue directly, offering support and encouraging the individual to seek help, thereby demonstrating a commitment to the well-being of your loved one, even when it's uncomfortable or risky.

Temperance

Temperance, or self-control, means regulating your desires and impulses to maintain a balanced life. It is achieved by practicing self-discipline and moderation in all aspects of life, ensuring that your desires don't overshadow reason and virtue.

Temperance Challenged

Imagine someone who struggles with anger management in personal relationships, who often reacts impulsively and regrets it later. The challenge to temperance is for them to recognize and control these impulses and to respond rather than react. Practicing temperance would involve learning to pause, reflect, and choose a more measured and constructive response when they are provoked, thereby maintaining harmony in their relationships and ensuring that their actions are aligned with their best self.

The Nine Core Stoic Beliefs

Embracing Stoicism's principles provides a foundation for a meaningful and balanced life. These teachings encourage you to prioritize rationality, ethical behavior, and inner peace. They guide your personal development and emotional intelligence, helping you understand your role in society and the universe. By adhering to these principles, you can strive for tranquility, resilience, and virtue and focus on ethical choices and personal growth. This path offers a way to navigate life's challenges with wisdom and composure.

The nine core beliefs that shape Stoic thought are:

- **Living according to nature:** Aligning life with nature's rational and harmonious order.

- **Virtue as the path to a good life:** Upholding goodness as the sole source of happiness.

- **The dichotomy of control:** Differentiating between what is and isn't within our control.

- **Inner resources:** Recognizing that all necessary resources for a good life are within us.

- **The art of living as a process:** Viewing life as a journey of continuous improvement.

- **Emotional control:** Managing emotions rather than being controlled by them.

- **Social philosophy of Stoics:** Emphasizing the interconnectedness and equality of all humans.

- **Cosmopolitanism:** Believing in a universal human community.

- **Universal reason (Logos):** Viewing the universe as a rational, orderly whole. (Hanselman, 2020)

Eudaemonia

In Stoicism, eudaemonia is understood as a state of flourishing or happiness that is achieved by living in accordance with reason and human nature. This concept is key to the philosophy, which suggests that it is attainable through the practice of virtue.

The Stoics view eudaemonia not as a fleeting emotion but as a stable and enduring state of being that results from living a life of moral integrity and wisdom and that is in harmony with the natural world. Achieving well-being involves accepting things outside of our control, embracing our fate, and striving to make the world a better place for all. This perspective on happiness is practical and focuses on rational thought and alignment with human nature.

To further your understanding of this state, it's essential to realize that it goes beyond mere happiness or pleasure. It's about achieving the highest human good by living a principled life (Van Treuren, n.d.). This includes practicing self-discipline, courage, justice, and wisdom. Stoics believe that by focusing on improving ourselves and acting with moral integrity, we naturally align ourselves with the universe's rational structure, leading to true fulfillment and well-being. This approach to happiness is deeply rooted in personal ethics and the betterment of our character.

The Triangle of Happiness

The Happiness Triangle is a way of understanding Stoic philosophy in a simple and easy-to-use framework. It focuses on three main ideas: being a good person, controlling what we can, and taking responsibility for how we react.

- **Living with areté:** This means expressing the best version of yourself in every moment and aligning your actions with your deep values.

- **Focusing on what you can control:** This involves concentrating on the aspects of life within your control and accepting the rest as it happens.

- **Taking responsibility:** This involves owning your judgments and responses to events and understanding that happiness or misery stems from your interpretations (Salzgeber, 2019).

The framework is significant because it visually portrays the interconnection and equilibrium of these three fundamental principles. Each side of the triangle relies on the others, indicating that these principles are interconnected and equally vital for attaining eudaemonia, or genuine happiness.

Key Stoic Philosophers

Zeno of Citium

Life

Zeno of Citium (ca. 336 B.C.E–265 B.C.E.), the founder of the Stoic school of philosophy in Athens, was born in Citium, a Phoenician-Greek city in Cyprus. His life coincided with Alexander the Great's ascension to the throne of Macedonia.

Inspired by his father who frequently traveled to Athens for work, Zeno first chose to become a merchant. However, at around the age of 22, after a shipwreck left him stranded in Athens, the young man's encounter with Xenophon's *Memorabilia,* a collection of Socratic dialogues, transformed his life, leading him to devote himself entirely to philosophy.

Renowned for his temperance and influential teachings, Zeno is reported to have ended his life by suicide following a trivial accident in which he broke his toe. The ancient philosopher took it as a sign and embodied the Stoic virtue of taking control over his destiny (Mark, 2014).

Thought

Zeno's philosophy encompassed various aspects of ethics, including the nature of good and bad, emotions, virtue, and actions. He argued that the ultimate goal in life is to live in harmony with nature, which is essentially the same as living virtuously.

According to Zeno, our individual natures are connected to the universal nature (Weaver, 2023b). He considered virtue to be a perfection that applies to all aspects of life, and he believed that it should be pursued for its own sake, regardless of external influences. Zeno also believed that virtue can be taught and that it includes both theoretical and practical elements.

Regrettably, none of Zeno's texts have survived. We do know that he authored a book, *Republic*, which presented opposing views to Plato's work with the same name.

Notable Quotes

- "Better to trip with the feet than with the tongue."

- "The reason why we have two ears and only one mouth is that we may listen the more and talk the less."

- "Man conquers the world by conquering himself."

- "Happiness is a good flow of life."

- "A bad feeling is a commotion of the mind, repugnant to reason and against nature."

- "Well-being is attained little by little and nevertheless is no little thing itself." (*Who Is Zeno?*, 2017)

Seneca the Younger

Life

Seneca the Younger, a prominent Stoic philosopher, was born into a wealthy Roman family in Corduba, Hispania (Weaver, 2023b). His early years were marked by an extensive education in Rome, where he was deeply influenced by Stoic teachings.

Despite facing exile and navigating the treacherous waters of Roman politics, including serving as an advisor to Nero, Seneca's contributions to philosophy remain his legacy. His life, characterized by both luxury and adversity, culminated in a forced suicide.

Thought

Seneca's philosophy is a testament to the Stoic ideals of virtue, reason, and self-control. He believed in living a life aligned with nature and logic, emphasizing moral integrity over material wealth. His thoughts on the human condition, ethics, and the nature of happiness have been influential. He advocated for a life of simplicity, duty, and reflection. His teachings focused on the development of personal virtue and the importance of inner tranquility.

Main Works

- *Epistulae Morales ad Lucilium* (*Letters From a Stoic*), which deliver philosophical counsel.

- *De Brevitate Vitae* (*On the Shortness of Life*), a text that ponders wise living.

- *De Ira* (*On Anger*), sheds insight on anger management.

- *De Providentia* (*On Providence*) discusses Stoic adversity.

Notable Quotes

- "We suffer more often in imagination than in reality."

- "Sometimes even to live is an act of courage."

- "You act like mortals in all that you fear, and like immortals in all that you desire."

- "As is a tale, so is life: not how long it is but how good it is, is what matters."

- "It is not the man who has too little but the man who craves more that is poor." (*Seneca Quotes*, n.d.)

Epictetus

Life

Epictetus (ca. 55 C.E.–135 C.E.) was either born into slavery or became enslaved in Phrygia. He was owned by Epaphroditus, a powerful figure in Nero's administration. Despite hardships, including physical disabilities, he pursued an education, with his owner's support, eventually gaining his freedom. Following being freed, Epictetus established a philosophy school in Greece and became renowned throughout the Roman Empire for his teachings and simplicity of living (Whelan, 2019).

Thought

Epictetus's teachings often revolved around practical advice for living a virtuous life. For example, he highlighted the importance of focusing only on what we can control, such as our actions and responses, rather than external events or the actions of others. This principle is vividly illustrated in his guidance on dealing with insults. Epictetus suggested that when someone insults you, it reflects more on their character than on yours. This teaches us the importance of maintaining inner peace and integrity in the face of external negativity. The example underscores his belief in the power of personal choice and reaction in shaping a life of virtue and tranquility.

Main Works

- *Discourses*, a collection of philosophical lectures on Stoicism.

- *Enchiridion*, a handbook for Stoic living.

Notable Quotes

- "No man is free who is not master of himself."

- "Who is your master? Anyone who has control over things upon which you've set your heart, or over things which you seek to avoid."

- "You are not your body and hairstyle, but your capacity for choosing well. If your choices are beautiful, so too will you be." (*Epictetus Quotes*, n.d.)

Gaius Musonius Rufus

Life

Gaius Musonius Rufus, born between 20 C.E. and 30 C.E., emerged as a leading Stoic philosopher in Imperial Rome. Dubbed the "Roman Socrates," Rufus's life was marked by his teachings, multiple exiles due to political dissent, and his significant influence on students like Epictetus (Weaver, 2023c).

Thought

Musonius Rufus championed Stoicism as a practical philosophy for everyday life, emphasizing virtue as the sole good. He believed in the equality of sexes in philosophical pursuit, the importance of education, and the embodiment of philosophy through action, not just theory. His teachings stressed living in accordance with nature and reason to achieve eudaemonia. The core lesson he imparted is that practical experience is more important than theoretical knowledge. Like Zeno, Rufus's contributions only survive through lectures and sayings recorded by his students.

Notable Quotes

- "What good are gilded rooms or precious stones fitted on the floor, inlaid in the walls, carried from great distances at the greatest expense? These things are pointless and unnecessary—without them isn't it possible to live healthy? Aren't they the source of constant trouble? Don't they cost vast sums of money that, through public and private charity, may have benefited many?"

- "Just as there is no use in medical study unless it leads to the health of the human body, so there is no use to a philosophical doctrine unless it leads to the virtue of the human soul."

- "You will earn the respect of all if you begin by earning the respect of yourself. Don't expect to encourage good deeds in people conscious of your own misdeeds."

- "The human being is born with an inclination toward virtue." (Daily Stoic, 2018)

Marcus Aurelius

Life

Marcus Aurelius, born into a prominent Roman family, became emperor of Rome in 161 C.E. and ruled until his death in 180 C.E. He was not initially in line for the throne but was adopted by Antoninus Pius, Emperor Hadrian's chosen successor. Becoming known as the last of the Five Good Emperors, Marcus Aurelius's reign was marked by challenges such as the Antonine Plague and conflicts with various tribes and nations (*Who Was Marcus Aurelius?*, n.d.).

Thought

Aurelius is celebrated for his philosophy, which emphasizes virtue, duty, and rationality. His approach to governance was informed by these principles, and he aimed for the welfare of his subjects and the stability of the Roman Empire. Stoicism guided him through personal and public crises, with its emphasis on acceptance and the importance of character (Daily Stoic, 2019).

Main Works

- *Meditations*

Notable Quotes

- "No carelessness in your actions. No confusion in your words. No imprecision in your thoughts." (Daily Stoic, 2019)

- "When the longest- and the shortest-lived of us come to die, their loss is precisely equal. For the sole thing of which any man can be deprived is the present; since this is all he owns, and nobody can lose what is not his." (*Who Was Marcus Aurelius?*, n.d.)

Mindfulness and Stoicism

Mindfulness, a concept often shrouded in simplicity yet profound in its depth, invites us into a state of active, open attention to the present. It is the practice of being fully engaged with whatever we're doing at any moment, free from distraction or judgment. It involves a kind of unattached awareness, where we observe our thoughts and feelings as they are, without trying to suppress or judge them.

This practice can be cultivated through various forms, including meditation, where you focus on your breath or a mantra, paying attention to the thoughts and sensations that arise and gently bringing your focus back whenever your mind wanders.

Stoicism intersects with mindfulness in its emphasis on awareness of the present moment and the control we have over our perceptions, judgments, and actions. Stoics like Marcus Aurelius, Seneca, and Epictetus taught the importance of focusing on the present, on what is within our power, and on accepting what is beyond our control. This fosters a tranquility that comes from within, irrespective of external circumstances. It encourages a life of virtue and reason.

The practice of mindfulness within Stoicism is not just about inner peace but also about living a life aligned with nature and reason. By being mindful, we can better understand our emotions, reduce our desires for what is beyond our control, and focus on our moral improvement.

This intersection between mindfulness and Stoicism offers a powerful framework for living a fulfilled life. The connection between the two highlights the importance of self-awareness, self-control, and ethical living. Through mindfulness, we can embody Stoic virtues, leading to a life that is not only more peaceful and content but also aligned with the highest good.

Interactive Element

Starting Your Own Stoic Journal Practice

As you delve into this book, you'll encounter journaling prompts that are more than just writing exercises; they are your stepping stones to practicing mindfulness in a way that intertwines seamlessly with Stoic philosophy. I invite you to engage deeply with these cues, using them as a mirror to reflect upon your thoughts, behaviors, and reactions without casting judgment. This isn't just about introspection. It's also an invitation to observe the ebb and flow of your inner life, to understand how your mind navigates the waters of daily existence.

Through engaging with these prompts, you're embarking on a journey to enhance your awareness of the present moment, to realign your actions with your deepest values, and to fully embrace the Stoic way of virtuous living. Think of journaling as channeling mindfulness by putting pen to paper, as a compass that guides you toward a deeper self-understanding and paves the way for a life marked by purpose, resilience, and a tranquil heart.

The connection between Stoicism and journaling lies in the cultivation of present-state awareness, self-reflection, and emotional resilience. Stoicism teaches us to focus on what we can control and accept things beyond our influence, while journaling helps us observe and understand our thoughts, actions, and reactions. By combining the two and using it as a method to delve into our actions and thoughts, we are able to uncover deeper insights. It allows us to have a meaningful conversation with ourselves and apply Stoic principles like inner resourcefulness, emotional control, and universal logic by fostering self-awareness and discipline (Nair, 2023a).

To make this experience truly your own, consider selecting a special journal dedicated to this purpose. It could be a beautifully bound notebook that appeals to your aesthetic sensibilities, a simple notepad that feels inviting and practical, or even a digital text document that offers convenience and flexibility. The choice of medium is yours and making it allows you to create a space that feels personal and conducive to your journaling practice.

The first exercise begins with the core principles of Stoicism and how they can be integrated into your daily reflections. As you learn more and go deeper into this practice, the subsequent chapters will unveil a variety of techniques designed to bolster your journaling efforts. Whether it's honing your ability to perceive events with clarity, fostering a sense of gratitude, or mastering your responses to life's challenges, there's a wealth of wisdom waiting to be discovered.

Explore how Stoic journaling can enhance our lives by following these prompts:

- **Control and acceptance:** Consider what's in your power to change and what isn't. How can you shift your focus to what you can control?

- **Facing challenges with Stoicism:** Reflect on a recent obstacle you faced. How did you handle it, and how might Stoic principles have led to a more positive result?

- **The power of gratitude:** Recall a moment when you could have shown more appreciation. How would expressing more gratitude have altered your view?

- **Cultivating a Stoic response:** Examine how you react to things outside your control. What steps can you take to develop a more Stoic attitude moving forward?

- **Living Stoically day by day:** Evaluate your everyday behavior. Does it reflect your core beliefs and the Stoic quest for moral excellence? If not, how can you improve on this?

Conclusion

As we come to the end of this chapter, we can reflect on how we have explored the profound wisdom of Stoic philosophy, which encourages us to understand the value of time and live with purpose and mindfulness. This ancient wisdom teaches us to be aware of the transient nature of life and prioritize actions that align with our fundamental beliefs rather than wasting our precious moments on trivial matters.

In the next chapter, we'll dive into the first letter of the VIRTUE framework that structures this book by exploring a crucial Stoic belief: That we must focus on what we can control and release what we can't. This idea guides us to put our energy and thoughts into our actions, responses, and feelings, steering clear of the fruitless effort to control the uncontrollable. We'll learn how to apply this wisdom in real life, gaining insights from Stoic thinkers on facing life's ups and downs with strength, building better relationships, and pursuing our goals with peace of mind.

Chapter Two

V: Veto the Uncontrollable

You have power over your mind—not outside events. Realize this, and you will find strength. –Marcus Aurelius

This first chapter in the VIRTUE framework starts with "V" for "veto the uncontrollable." Here, we will emphasize the importance of not letting the uncontrollable aspects of life consume us.

This concept can be outlined by considering the example of a smartphone that alerts you of new messages or app reminders. Some of these notifications you can adjust and personalize, while others occur automatically through fixed settings outside your direct control. When the software updates or you get a newer model, there will be new features that may be frustrating. You didn't choose them, and you can't alter them.

Dwelling on every difference and agonizing over new features or modifications to the device's interface—or your life—can lead to a cycle of frustration and distraction. However, there is value in acknowledging these updates as inevitable developments that mark a step forward in the evolution of your digital companion. This acceptance empowers you to focus your energies on mastering the aspects that are within your sphere of control.

Stoics on the Dichotomy of Control

In the words of Epictetus (n.d.):

There are things which are within our power, and there are things which are beyond our power. Within our power are opinion, aim, desire, aversion, and, in one word, whatever affairs are our own. Beyond our power are body, property, reputation, office, and, in one word, whatever are not properly our own affairs.

Understanding the dichotomy of control is crucial for peace of mind. As Epictetus has stated, it's pointless to worry over things you cannot change, and when something is within your scope of influence, worry is unnecessary because you can change it.

The Stoic principle of the dichotomy of control therefore guides you to focus on what you can manage—your thoughts, decisions, and actions—while accepting what you cannot, like others' actions or societal trends (Weaver, 2019b). It aims to reduce stress by promoting a focus on personal virtue and growth, teaching you to discern between changeable aspects and those that you have to accept as they are. Embracing this mindset leads to deeper fulfillment, not from external accolades but from developing resilience and virtue amid life's unpredictability.

Virtue vs. Fortune

Epictetus encourages you to recognize that true goodness lies in cultivating virtues like wisdom, courage, justice, and self-discipline—qualities completely within your control. Unlike external factors such as wealth, health, and social status, which are unpredictable and beyond your influence, focusing on your values can lead to genuine happiness and freedom.

It's like getting ready for a big presentation: Your main goal is to prepare thoroughly, but you know that your audience's final reaction is unpredictable. This example shows that, while you can manage your preparation and effort, the outcome is not always in your hands. In everything you do, there are aspects you can influence (such as the depth of research or the time you put into rehearsing what you want to say) and aspects you cannot (like the general mood in the room or individual interest levels).

The key takeaway is that, although you aim for positive results, your sense of value shouldn't hinge on uncertain outcomes. The amount of effort you put in is within your control, but the results often will not be. Adopting calm acceptance of outcomes regardless of whether or not they are successful represents the most balanced approach to life.

Examples of the Dichotomy of Control in Everyday Life

- **Career progression:** In your career, you can determine how much effort you put into your work, your willingness to learn new skills, and your attitude toward challenges. However, your boss' decisions, company policies, and market trends are beyond your control. Living in alignment with Stoic principles means focusing on your personal development and response to feedback rather than obsessing over promotions or recognition.

- **Relationships:** You can strive to be understanding, patient, and supportive in your relationships, but you cannot control the feelings or actions of others. Accepting this can help you maintain your peace of mind and focus on being the best version of yourself rather than trying to change someone else.

- **Health and fitness:** While you can control your diet, exercise routine, and lifestyle choices, some health issues may arise due to genetics or unforeseen circumstances. The Stoic approach here is to focus on maintaining your healthy habits rather than focusing on trying to avoid the outcomes that may arise.

Embracing the Uncontrollable: Stoicism, Buddhism, and the Art of Navigating Life

Philosophers are known for their comprehensive exploration of ideas and for always striving to understand every facet of an argument or theory. This thorough approach ensures a balanced and nuanced understanding of complex topics. In the spirit of fairness and intellectual rigor, comparing Stoicism to other philosophical theories provides a broader perspective on life's challenges, how they may be perceived, and the various strategies for addressing them. In this case, it's enlightening to juxtapose Stoicism with other philosophies such as existentialism and Buddhism.

Stoicism tells us to focus on what we can control like our thoughts, actions, and attitudes. This helps us feel empowered and calm in the face of what we can't influence, like what others do or what happens in society. It emphasizes personal virtue, resilience, and the importance of accepting life's unpredictability with a calm mind.

Existentialism, with its emphasis on individual existence, delves into the significance of freedom, choice, and responsibility. Unlike Stoicism, which advises acceptance of external circumstances, this philosophical movement encourages us to create our own meaning in a seemingly indifferent universe. It suggests that through the exercise of free will and personal decision-making, we can navigate the absurdity of life and assert our essence.

On the other hand, Buddhism teaches us about impermanence and posits that everything in life is always changing. Its teachings advise us to be okay with this transience. It encourages us to let go of our need to hold on to things or push them away, which can be the cause of a lot of our suffering. Buddhism helps us see that everything, including our own experiences, doesn't last forever—a lesson that can help us find peace even when things are tough.

Defining Your Sphere of Control

Incorporating the dichotomy of control into your life means recognizing what is within your grasp: your behaviors, choices, and responses. Channel your energy into developing your character and your reactions to life's challenges. Embrace the aspects of life beyond your influence with serenity. This strategy is not about resignation but about directing your efforts to where they can genuinely effect change, leading to a life marked by tranquility and empowerment.

To put this into practice, consider starting each day by contemplating the upcoming events and distinguishing what you can determine, like your actions and attitudes, from what you can't, such as others' words and unexpected occurrences. Keep these differences in mind, particularly when you encounter obstacles or stressors. Making this a habit aids in concentrating your energy on constructive activities and preserving a calm state of mind despite unpredictability. It also encourages a pattern of reacting to circumstances with insight and balance, promoting self-development and resilience.

As your day unfolds, consciously decide where to focus your attention and energy. When you are faced with hurdles or choices, question whether the matter is within your control. If it is, act decisively and take responsibility for your reactions. If it is not, learn to release it, concentrating instead on how you can evolve and learn from the situation. This change in outlook will help you alleviate stress, and it deepens your sense of peace and satisfaction.

Adopting this perspective further facilitates self-improvement. By concentrating on what you can influence—your thoughts, perspectives, and deeds—you lay the groundwork for personal advancement. Obstacles will transform into chances to prove your resilience and flexibility. This life philosophy doesn't merely reduce avoidable stress; it boosts your capacity to flourish amid change, rendering you more robust and ready for the future.

Goal-Setting Strategies: Empowering Your Sphere of Control

Incorporating Stoicism into your life isn't just about accepting what you can't control; it's also about actively shaping what you can. A powerful tool in this endeavor is the art of setting goals—and not just any goals but those that are finely tuned to fall within your sphere of control. This is where specific, measurable, achievable, relevant, and time-bound (SMART) goals come into play. By setting your goals in line with these criteria, you can focus on what truly matters and what you can influence, which is in line with Stoic wisdom. Here is a breakdown of each component of this framework:

- **Specific:** Your goals should be clear and specific without any ambiguity about what you aim to achieve. Instead of setting a goal to be happier, define what happiness means to you in actionable terms, such as "to spend 30 minutes a day on a hobby that I love."

- **Measurable:** Make sure your goal is quantifiable so that you can track your progress. For example, if your goal is to reduce stress, a measurable version could be, "I will practice 10 minutes of meditation, five days a week."

- **Achievable:** Your goals should be realistic and attainable with your current resources and constraints. While it's good to be ambitious, aiming too high can lead to frustration. If you're new to meditation, a goal of "attaining enlightenment through meditation in one month" is less achievable than "learning and practicing mindfulness meditation for the next four weeks."

- **Relevant:** Ensure your goals are relevant to your personal values and long-term objectives. This alignment guarantees that your efforts are meaningful and contribute to your overall sense of purpose and fulfillment. If one of your values is lifelong learning, a relevant goal could be "to read one book related to Stoicism each month."

- **Time-bound:** Every goal needs a target date so that you know when to evaluate your progress. A goal with a time limit commits you to a deadline, creating a sense of urgency and motivation. For instance, "complete a 5K run in under 30 minutes by the end of the season" is a goal with a clear timeframe.

Mastering Self-Control

Stoics emphasized discipline and self-control, both of which are achievable through:

- Mastering our impulses and focusing on what's within our control.

- Practicing meditation, reflection, and virtuous living.

- Utilizing our reason over our emotions and desires.

- Accepting fate while striving for personal excellence.

- Conducting self-examinations and learning from our role models.

- Viewing the challenges that face us as opportunities for growth.

Putting these actions into practice is achievable. You can start by developing self-mastery and temperance, which can be done by taking small, disciplined actions to build resilience. Additionally, you can reflect nightly on these steps while also learning from those wiser than yourself. By taking the time to do this, you can gain a better sense of self-awareness and a more balanced perspective. Adopting the habit of nightly reflections shows that you are making a conscious effort to grow and develop each day, allowing you to cultivate a sense of persistence and adaptability.

In your daily life, understand that distractions are within your control. Learning how to manage them can greatly improve your ability to stay focused on the tasks at hand as well as your goals. With clear focus, you will see that every day offers a new opportunity for growth. So, concentrate on the present, question your judgments, accept what you cannot change, and strive to conquer your desires. Practicing these actions has the additional benefit of helping you promote your emotional regulation. Additionally, mastering your immediate desires can help you better align your actions with your long-term ambitions instead of giving in to immediate impulses.

These activities help you strengthen your self-control by building up your willpower, much like how muscles are developed with regular exercise. Through meditation, reflection, and moderation, you can live a life guided by wisdom and virtue, achieving tranquility and control over your path.

Simple Steps for a More Controlled Life

By weaving some simple practices into your daily life, you can start embodying the essence of Stoicism tangibly and meaningfully. Each action is crafted to be both achievable and gradual, enabling small yet significant changes to your lifestyle.

- **Start your day with morning reflections:** Dedicate the first five minutes of your morning to thinking about what's within your control and what isn't. Reflect on your goals for the day ahead and recognize the external factors you cannot change. This sets a purposeful tone for your day, aligning your actions with Stoic wisdom.

- **Embrace minor discomforts:** Strengthen your willpower by choosing to face small discomforts voluntarily. Try taking a cold shower or fasting for part of the day, if it's safe for you to do. These acts of self-discipline remind you of the difference between wants and needs, fostering a Stoic resilience against discomfort.

- **Unplug with digital detoxes:** Carve out times each day to step away from all digital screens. Whether you do it during meals, an hour before bed, or a specific afternoon break, adopting this practice helps you regain control over your attention and reduces your reactivity to incessant notifications.

- **Perform daily acts of kindness:** Make it a daily goal to do something kind for someone without expecting anything in return. This practice is deeply Stoic, as it focuses on actions you can control—your generosity and kindness—thus enriching your sense of community and connection.

- **Reflect in the evening:** Spend a few minutes each night journaling about the day's events. Focus on distinguishing between what was within your control and what was not. This reflection helps cultivate a mindset that values personal responsibility and acceptance of life's unpredictability.

- **Set and review achievable goals:** Regularly set small, realistic personal development goals and check your progress. This keeps you focused on self-improvement, which is within your sphere of influence, thereby embodying the Stoic commitment to continuous growth and self-reflection.

- **Practice mindful consumption:** Be aware of what you consume, whether it's food, information, or entertainment. Choosing consciously based on your values and well-being rather than on whims or impulses is a practice in Stoic self-control and virtue.

Locus of Control: Taking Charge of Your Own Destiny

Internal vs. External Locus of Control

Your locus of control shapes how you view your ability to influence the events in your life. If you lean toward an internal locus of control, you believe your actions have a direct impact on their outcomes, crediting your successes to your efforts and skills. On the flip side, an external locus of control means you see what happens in your life as mostly out of your hands, driven by outside forces or luck (Camp, 2020). Understanding where you stand is key to your personal growth, influencing your motivation, self-esteem, and how you tackle life's challenges and opportunities.

The idea of the locus of control aligns well with the fundamental principles of Stoicism. In essence, if you adopt an internal locus of control, much like the Stoics did, you understand that your actions, thoughts, and emotions are within your power to influence. This serves as a vital aspect of living a Stoic life, where the aim is to attain tranquility by devoting attention to your own efforts and attitudes rather than being influenced by external factors beyond your control. It entails recognizing where your true power lies and utilizing it wisely.

Developing Your Locus of Control

To develop and make the most out of your internal locus of control, focus on recognizing and strengthening your sense of personal agency. Part of this journey involves accepting and letting go of what is unchangeable and directing your energy toward areas of your life where you can make a real impact.

By contemplating questions that encourage introspection and proactive decision-making, you can begin to identify areas where you can exert more influence, leading to enhanced self-awareness and a more proactive approach to life. Some questions you can ask yourself are:

- What recent decision did I make that significantly affected my life, and what was its impact?

- What are the core values that guide my actions, and how do they influence my sense of control?

- Can I identify a moment where I felt powerless, and what steps could I have taken to change the outcome?

- What habits or behaviors do I believe are holding me back from achieving my goals, and how can I address them?

- How do I react to unexpected challenges, and what can I do to respond more proactively in the future?

Embracing Stoicism in Modern Life: The Power of Internal Control and Mindfulness

Stoicism, with its focus on controlling our internal states rather than allowing ourselves to be swayed by external circumstances, offers timeless wisdom for modern living. Research validates the importance of adopting this perspective.

Studies reveal that when you set personal goals, tapping into your internal locus of control, your engagement and success rates climb (Lambert et al., 1999). Models for improving self-control, as outlined in Inzlicht et al.'s 2014 paper titled "Exploring the Mechanisms of Self-Control Improvement," also align with Stoic practices, highlighting the significance of setting meaningful goals and ensuring your actions reflect these ambitions. Additionally, findings demonstrate that possessing an internal locus of control is linked to positive work outcomes, reinforcing the Stoic principle of focusing on personal power (Ng et al., 2006).

The acknowledgment of your ability to influence outcomes, particularly in settings like therapy, underscores the power of personal agency and further mirrors Stoic advice (Mitchell, 1989). The validity of this finding is bolstered by studies that have found that there is a connection between feeling in control of your life and experiencing less stress. According to Isaacs, as expressed in a 2023 article published in *The Journal of Paediatrics and Child Health*, this is known as the "status effect."

Furthermore, researchers have concluded that mindfulness can enhance your resilience, boost your self-esteem, and strengthen your sense of power, thereby diminishing negative emotions and promoting a positive outlook (Dong et al., 2022). Finally, explorations into Stoic philosophy in areas like genetic counseling show its potential to help you develop a rational, healthy internal locus of control, aiding in managing responses to life's uncontrollable events (Crawford & Helm, 2019).

<hr />

Interactive Element

Dichotomy of Control Meditation

This meditation encourages you to identify what you can control—your actions and reactions—and accept what you cannot. Through its focus on deep breathing and reflection, it guides you toward distinguishing your influence from the uncontrollable, fostering acceptance and gratitude.

1. **Find a quiet space:** Choose a peaceful location where you can sit comfortably for about 10-15 minutes without interruptions.

2. **Focus on your breath:** Begin by taking deep, slow breaths. Inhale through your nose, hold for a moment, and exhale through your mouth. This helps to center your mind and body.

3. **Reflect on what's within your control:** Think about aspects of your life that you can determine, such as your thoughts, actions, and reactions. Acknowledge these areas, focusing on the power you have over your responses to external events.

4. **Acknowledge what's beyond your control:** Now, shift your focus to things outside your influence—other people's actions, natural events, or the past. Recognize these elements without attaching emotions or judgments to them.

5. **Separate your impressions from their sources:** As thoughts and feelings arise during the meditation, especially regarding things outside your control, consciously separate your initial impressions from the actual events. Recognize that you can mold your interpretation of an event, even if the event itself is not within your power to influence.

6. **Reflect on a challenging event:** Think about a recent obstacle in your life. Observe your initial reactions and feelings toward it. Use this as an opportunity to practice separating your impressions from the incident itself and recognize what aspects of the situation were within your control and what aspects were not. Consider how you can choose your response to similar future occurrences, focusing on how your actions and attitudes can address the challenge constructively.

7. **Return gently:** Bring your focus back to your breath, then to your surroundings. Open your eyes when you are ready, carrying this mindset into your daily life.

8. **Set intentions:** Conclude the exercise by setting intentions based on your reflections. Decide how you will respond to both controllable and uncontrollable aspects of life moving forward.

9. **Cultivate gratitude:** For what is within your sphere of influence, express gratitude as this strengthens your appreciation and acceptance, enhancing your emotional well-being.

10. **Embrace acceptance:** As you differentiate between the two realms, practice accepting what you cannot determine. Feel any tension or resistance you have toward these external factors dissipate as you breathe out.

Applying Stoic Wisdom

Victor E. Frankl's assertion that "when we are no longer able to change a situation, we are challenged to change ourselves" reflects the Stoic attitude discussed throughout this chapter. The sentiment can be applied in all areas of your life, including the professional domain. For example, when you encounter a major obstacle at work like a key project being scrapped, it can be incredibly disheartening.

When an event like this happens, your hard work might seem wasted, but it's crucial to remember that your power lies in your mindset and reactions, not the challenges that occur. This understanding is vital for navigating through the unpredictability of professional life. If you respond to this setback by analyzing what happened and focusing on your contributions and teamwork, you highlight what you can change. The project's cancellation, possibly due to budget constraints or strategic changes, is out of your hands.

By acknowledging this separation between what you can and cannot influence, you shift your focus from what was lost to the valuable lessons and skills you've gained. This approach isn't about undermining the setback's impact but about realizing where your true power lies—in how you react and adapt. You begin to view the canceled project not as a failure but as a chance to improve your methods and prepare for future opportunities with more insight and resilience.

Moving forward, you can approach a new challenge with a stronger grasp of Stoicism's core virtues: wisdom, courage, justice, and self-discipline. You can concentrate on what you can influence—your dedication, creativity, and contribution to teamwork—while accepting the outcome's uncertainty with a sense of calm.

This change in perspective will lead your colleagues to see you as not just competent but as a resilient and adaptable leader, capable of handling adversity with grace and determination. Your Stoic approach to challenges can inspire your team, creating a culture of fortitude and growth.

When you reflect on your experiences, you will recognize that the most profound change has been within yourself. The setback served as a trigger for your personal development, pushing you toward a better understanding of yourself and your capabilities. Looking back, you will see that by focusing on what you could shape, you have become more effective at your job, and you will have found a deeper sense of peace and fulfillment.

Conclusion

In this chapter, we have looked into the idea of focusing on what we can control—our thoughts, choices, and actions—instead of what's beyond our reach. However, we have also established that the Stoic dichotomy of control does not advocate for passive acceptance but for dynamic engagement with life, where virtue is our compass and wisdom is our sail.

As you have seen, the "V" for "veto" represents our ability to reject the premise that external circumstances dictate our happiness and well-being. We have rejected the notion that we are passive recipients of fate, instead embracing the power we possess over our perceptions, intentions, and reactions. Moving to the "I" for "ideal self" involves a more intricate and positive assertion of our capabilities. It will be about identifying, envisioning, and striving toward an embodiment of Stoic ideals in our personal character and daily lives.

Moving forward, it's important to understand that learning to be aware of ourselves and practicing self-discipline is just the starting point, not the end goal. The next chapter will build on this idea. It will encourage us to see ourselves as artists, as the pursuit of personal excellence invites us to envision ourselves as sculptors. As you will learn, Stoicism provides the tools for us to chisel away the superfluous, revealing the best versions of ourselves beneath.

CHAPTER THREE

I: INSPIRE YOUR IDEAL SELF

I will keep constant watch over myself and—most useful-ly—will put each day up for review. For this is what makes us evil—that none of us looks back upon our own lives. We reflect upon only that which we are about to do. And yet our plans for the future descend from the past. –Seneca

Now that you have learned about accepting the limitations of your control, we can shift your focus from chasing external validation to nurturing your inner virtues. In the VIRTUE framework that structures this book, this chapter represents the "I," referring to your ideal self. In this sense, "ideal" is not about perfection but about continuous growth, self-improvement, and alignment with your values and purpose.

It's essential to have a guiding light, and Stoic philosophy provides the guidance you need as you embark on the quest to discover the best version of yourself. This path goes beyond just making small improvements in your life. It involves a profound change that touches the core of who you are. This kind of transformation requires you to live with absolute integrity, genuinely living out the values that are important to you. It's a journey that requires you to take small, consistent steps every day.

Seneca's Teachings

This section explores Seneca's wisdom on personal development. His thought is particularly relevant, as his teachings emphasize the transformative power of self-reflection. Notably, Seneca framed introspection as a personal courtroom where you stand as both judge and defendant over your actions and thoughts (Harte, 2022). From this unique perspective, self-examination, which is pivotal in forging a path toward your ideal self, is about learning from your past errors.

Seneca proposes moderation and self-discipline as ways to value simplicity and resilience, emphasizing preparation for adversity. He also highlights the crucial alignment between actions and words, urging the application of Stoic principles in everyday life.

He advocates for showing wisdom through actions rather than discussions and striving for consistency in our behavior to reflect Stoic ideals of living true to our teachings. However, Seneca acknowledges the challenge of this alignment in a letter he writes to Gaius Lucilius, a Roman satirist, wherein he attributes inconsistencies to not earnestly pursuing virtue (*Letter XX*, 2020).

Seneca critiques the ineffectiveness of half-hearted commitments to virtue, pointing out the distractions of seeking external rewards like wealth or status. He suggests true happiness and freedom stem from rejecting material success and focusing on virtue. This pursuit, he warns, often leads to self-imposed bondage, with individuals losing sight of true values due to their desires and societal pressures.

Discussing noble goals, Seneca stresses the importance of prioritizing wisdom and virtue over indulging in pleasures and material gains. He champions a life driven by moral excellence, critiquing the societal focus on luxury and economic achievements. He warns against enslavement to desires, advocating for a simpler, integrity-filled life.

Seneca delves into the divine presence within us that guides our moral choices and actions. Acknowledging and respecting this inner divinity, he argues, leads to virtuous living. He connects this concept with the awe nature inspires, suggesting such experiences reflect our internal godliness and urging a life aligned with our true essence and inner guidance.

Challenging the abstraction of virtue, Seneca posits that virtue is tangible and evidenced through actions affecting our mental and physical states. This view links the physical and moral realms, asserting the realness of spiritual and personal values as much as our physical existence.

Seneca examines human imperfections, likening spiritual and moral shortcomings to physical sickness. He argues for increased self-awareness and philosophical commitment to identify and mend these flaws. True growth, he suggests, comes from a deep self-examination and a dedication to fostering virtue; it is akin to the care for a severe illness.

In his exploration of the nature of virtue as the ultimate good, Seneca maintains that being honorable and unaffected by external changes stands above all perceived good. He encourages fully embracing our principles, assuring us that doing so equips us to transform adversities into opportunities for strengthening our character and for positive outcomes.

In our quest for the ideal self, understanding and cultivating practical wisdom, or *phronesis*, becomes indispensable. This ancient Greek concept, deeply rooted in both Stoic and Aristotelian philosophy, refers to the ability to make good judgments and decisions that align with our ethical beliefs and values in the complex and often unpredictable landscape of human life. It is not merely theoretical knowledge; it is also a deeply ingrained practical skill that guides us in acting virtuously in the myriad situations we encounter daily.

Practical wisdom involves more than just knowing what is right; it also involves applying that knowledge in real-world scenarios to navigate toward the best possible outcomes. It requires an acute awareness of the nuances of each situation, the ability to deliberate on possible actions, and the insight to foresee their consequences. At its core, phronesis empowers us to balance our immediate desires with our long-term goals, helping us to act consistently with our deeper values and principles.

Developing practical wisdom is a dynamic process that evolves through experience, reflection, and a deliberate practice of virtue. It starts with self-awareness—understanding our values, strengths, and weaknesses. From this foundation, we can begin to observe and learn from the decisions we make, especially those that lead to meaningful outcomes, both positive and negative.

The cultivation of practical wisdom profoundly impacts our pursuit of the ideal self. It enhances our ability to make decisions that not only serve our immediate interests but also contribute to our overall well-being and fulfillment. By acting with phronesis, we embody the virtues that define our character, leading to a life that is not only ethically grounded but also deeply satisfying.

In our journey toward personal excellence and embodying our ideal selves, the community around us plays a pivotal role, mirroring the Stoic view of interconnectedness and reflecting the remarkable impact of external relationships on internal growth. Additionally, Stoicism, with its emphasis on virtue, wisdom, and self-improvement, also recognizes the significant influence that our social environment and relationships have on our development.

Self-improvement holds a central place in Stoicism, and it is regarded as the pathway to attaining virtue, which is seen as the highest good and the basis for a fulfilling life.

Stoicism teaches the importance of self-awareness, resilience, and the pursuit of wisdom, aligning closely with the steps toward crafting and evolving your ideal self-image. Discovering your ideal self involves first assessing your current self-image, which is crucial for setting a direction for personal growth.

By adopting Stoic principles, you gain the ability to face life's obstacles with wisdom and resilience, ultimately leading you toward a path of personal excellence. Embarking on this journey toward self-improvement can also boost your confidence and reduce anxiety, leading to an increase in motivation and a sense of fulfillment.

So, what does your ideal self look like?

This question is essential to Stoicism, but it can be answered using modern guidance. For example, Eli Straw (2023) emphasizes the importance of crafting a version of yourself you aim to be and aspire toward in all your goals. His advice highlights the need for self-evaluation and recognizing areas for improvement.

The first part of the process of putting this into action requires you to envision how you want to see yourself in various areas of your life. You may want to be more confident, be more productive at work, or strengthen your personal relationships. The next part involves taking tangible steps toward these aspirations through goal setting and visualization techniques.

As you go along, you will discover that crafting an ideal self-image is a dynamic process. In this philosophical context, this version of yourself is not a static end goal but a horizon that recedes as you advance, always calling you to higher standards of being and acting in the world. Your ideal self continually evolves as you experience personal growth. The measure of your progress, therefore, lies not in the distance covered but in the depth of your engagement with the questions that define your humanity.

The quest for an ideal self raises fundamental questions about the essence of personal identity and the ethical imperatives that guide our transformation. What constitutes this ideal, and who determines its contours? Is it a reflection of societal expectations, a personal aspiration untouched by external influences, or a blend of both?

Philosophically, the pursuit of an ideal self can be seen as a journey toward eudaemonia. Aristotle used this term to describe a state of being wherein we live in accordance with virtue, fulfilling our potentialities to the fullest. This journey is not merely about achieving external markers of success but involves a profound engagement with our values, actions, and purpose. It necessitates a dialogue between us and our conception of the good life, where the person we aspire to be becomes a compass guiding our ethical conduct and personal excellence.

Determining this self, then, is an existential endeavor, one that requires introspection and a willingness to confront the complexities of our nature. It involves asking yourself: What virtues do I hold dear? What legacy do I wish to leave? How do my actions align with my deepest values?

To start becoming the best version of yourself, you need to change your way of thinking, be determined, and believe in your ability to control your thoughts and actions. To do this, try these easy practices inspired by Stoicism.

Stoic philosophy, as epitomized by Seneca, teaches us to see time as our most valuable asset. It urges us to protect and use it wisely, much like we would safeguard our most prized possessions. Seneca's teachings emphasize the importance of being mindful of how we spend our time, urging us to focus on what truly matters and to avoid procrastination to live a life full of meaning.

In this framework, the urgency to live a virtuous life is central. It's about seizing each day with intention and recognizing that our time here is limited. This is not about dwelling on the end of life but rather an encouragement to live fully and meaningfully, making the best of the time we have. The idea is to reflect regularly on whether our daily actions are aligned with the legacy we aim to leave, encouraging us to concentrate on what's genuinely important—developing virtues, acting ethically, and cherishing the present moment. Such mindfulness leads to a deeper engagement with life as it unfolds, guiding our aspirations away from fleeting joys or external validations and toward a continuous journey of seeking wisdom and ethical excellence.

By integrating these principles into our lives, we not only prepare ourselves for life's inevitable conclusion but also enhance our path toward self-improvement, making every decision and moment meaningful. To embody this philosophy and make the most out of every moment, aiming for a life defined by fulfillment and virtue, consider adopting the following strategies:

- **Live deliberately:** Make conscious choices about how you spend your time, focusing on activities that align with your values and goals.

- **Prioritize wisely:** Identify what is most important in your life and allocate your time and resources accordingly.

- **Practice mindfulness:** Engage fully with the present moment, whether you're working, spending time with loved ones, or enjoying solitude.

- **Cultivate virtue:** Focus on personal growth and moral improvement, aiming to be the best version of yourself.

- **Eliminate distractions:** Minimize activities and influences that waste your time or detract from your life's purpose.

- **Reflect regularly:** Take time to contemplate your actions and choices, ensuring they reflect the legacy you wish to create.

Staying on the Upward Path

Embarking on a personal growth journey can be both exhilarating and challenging. Staying motivated throughout this process is crucial for achieving your goals and realizing your potential. This FAQ is designed to address common questions and provide actionable advice to help you maintain your incentive, overcome obstacles, and make meaningful progress. Whether you're struggling to find motivation, set achievable goals, or need strategies to keep a positive mindset, these insights aim to guide you on your path to personal growth, integrating timeless wisdom with practical steps.

FAQ: Staying Motivated on Your Personal Growth Journey

Q: How can I find my motivation for personal growth?

A: Understand your core reasons and what truly drives you. This foundational understanding fuels your perseverance.

Q: What's the best way to set goals for personal growth?

A: Break your main goals into smaller, manageable tasks to make progress feel more achievable.

Q: How can I maintain a positive mindset?

A: Surround yourself with positivity and people who uplift and support your growth journey.

Q: What should I do if I'm too hard on myself?

A: Practice self-compassion. Be kind to yourself, acknowledging both your efforts and the challenges you face.

Q: How can I start when I'm not feeling motivated?

A: Try the 10-minute rule. Commit to your goal for just 10 minutes and do so repeatedly to build momentum.

Q: How should I celebrate my progress?

A: Reward yourself for any progress, no matter how small, to maintain your motivation.

Q: What if I need help or support?

A: Don't hesitate to seek help from friends and family or join support groups related to your goals.

Q: What if my goals no longer feel right?

A: Regularly review and adjust your goals. Being flexible allows you to stay aligned with your evolving aspirations.

Interactive Element

Five-Minute Daily Self-Reflection Habit

In the hustle and bustle of daily life, taking a moment for personal reflection can seem like a luxury we can't afford. Yet the ancient practice of Stoicism teaches us that such moments are essential to understanding ourselves and living a life of purpose and fulfillment. By dedicating just five minutes a day to self-reflection, we can unlock a deeper awareness of our actions, emotions, and the choices that shape our lives.

In Chapter 1, we set the foundation for a journaling practice that facilitates reflection based on the principles of Stoic philosophy. Establishing a daily habit of self-reflection starts with setting aside a consistent time each day, such as in the morning or right before bed, and making it an official part of your schedule by adding it to your calendar. To capture spontaneous insights and reflections throughout the day, keep your notebook or digital note-taking device within reach. Begin your reflection sessions with guiding questions to direct your focus:

- **What is enough?** This question prompts you to consider your needs versus wants, encouraging contentment and gratitude for what you have.

- **Did you act according to the four virtues of Stoicism today?** Reflect on whether your actions fostered personal growth and ethical living by aligning with the Stoic virtues of wisdom, justice, courage, and temperance.

- **Will anger make this better or worse?** Answering this question encourages examination of your emotions and their impact on situations, promoting a rational response over an emotional reaction.

- **Did you enjoy the good things today, acknowledging that nothing lasts forever?** Use this as a reminder of the impermanence of life and the importance of appreciating the present moment.

- **Are you being a good friend to yourself?** Allow the process of addressing this to promote self-compassion and understanding and encourage a kind and forgiving attitude toward yourself.

- **Did you practice mindfulness today?** Focus on building your self-awareness and living in the present when you approach this question, as it can enhance your personal well-being and reduce stress.

Applying Stoic

Wisdom

Recently, I came across the following quote by Norman Vincent Peale: "Change your thoughts and you change your world."

It inspired me to take action in my life, so I decided to give Seneca's advice a real shot. It was surprisingly straightforward—I took just a few minutes each night to jot down thoughts. So, here I am with my reflections. For me, this isn't about deep soul-searching but more like taking a step back to see where I'm at versus where I want to be.

This journaling thing is pretty simple but eye-opening. It helps me catch myself when I'm about to go off track. By recording my thoughts, I've come to see that chasing after what I thought was success or looking for approval from others isn't really what's going to fulfill me. Rather, it's more about aligning my daily actions with what I genuinely value.

Paying attention to how I spend my time was another game-changer. I started being pickier about what I would say yes to and making room for things that matter to me. It was easier than I thought to ditch stuff that wasn't adding value to my life. This small change alone has made my days feel more meaningful.

My ambitions have shifted, too. Instead of being obsessed with hitting certain milestones or accumulating material objects, I'm now more interested in my personal growth and acting with integrity. It's refreshing to feel like I'm on a path that resonates with who I want to be.

It turns out that applying Stoicism to daily life isn't complicated. It's about making small adjustments, like taking a moment to reflect, choosing where to focus my energy, and remembering what's actually in my control. This practice has been more helpful than I expected. It's keeping me grounded and focused on what matters.

So, as I continue this journaling habit, it's becoming clear that these aren't just philosophical musings but practical steps that are helping me inch closer to the person I aim to be. It's not about perfection but progress, and surprisingly, it's not as daunting as I thought it would be.

Conclusion

As we close this chapter on the ideal self, we've delved deep into exploring the Stoic pursuit of virtue and the alignment of our actions with deeply held values. We've examined the importance of living with integrity, the pursuit of wisdom, and the cultivation of our principles.

As you embark on this journey of self-improvement, remember: Your path is uniquely yours. Seneca's wisdom isn't just about adopting a set of practices; it's about embracing a mindset of growth, resilience, and integrity. Reflect daily, not just on what you plan to do but on what you've achieved and learned. Let virtue guide your actions, seek wisdom in every challenge, and remember to be a friend to yourself. Your efforts today are the foundation of the person you aspire to be tomorrow. Embrace this journey with an open heart, knowing each step forward is a step toward becoming your best self.

Moving on, the next chapter delves into the concept of amor fati, a powerful Stoic principle that calls on us to fully embrace and find contentment in our current situations. It encourages us to see the beauty in our unique stories, urging us to accept life's unfolding with grace and resilience. You will learn how to find amor fati in your heart, thereby fostering your profound acceptance of life as it is. We will also highlight the serenity that comes from embracing every moment of your journey.

Your Words Can Spark Change

Small acts of kindness can lead to big changes. - Unknown

Imagine if every time we learned something new, we shared it with someone else. Think of how much brighter and stronger our world would be! That's exactly what we're aiming to do with *Stoic Philosophy for Beginners*.

So, here's an interesting idea...

What if your thoughts and experiences could really make a difference in someone else's life?

Imagine someone just like you, not too long ago—curious, searching for guidance, and ready to take on life's challenges. They're out there, hoping to find the same kind of wisdom and strength you've discovered.

Our dream is to share the timeless lessons of Stoic Philosophy with everyone. But, we can't do it alone. We need your help to spread this wisdom far and wide.

You know, lots of folks decide whether a book is worth their time based on what other readers have to say. That's why I'm reaching out to you for a small favor on behalf of someone you haven't met yet:

Would you consider leaving a review for our book?

This little act of kindness—taking less than a minute of your time and not costing a penny—could transform another person's life in more ways than we can count. Your review might just help someone...

...navigate through tough times with grace.

...learn the power of focusing on what they can control.

...discover inner strength they never knew they had.

...feel encouraged on their journey of self-improvement.

...embrace a life filled with more happiness and less worry.

Eager to share a bit of goodness and wisdom? It's easy to leave your review here:

Just scan the QR code to start sharing your valuable insights.

If you're moved by the idea of guiding someone towards a more resilient and joyful life, then you're our kind of person. Welcome to our community! You play a crucial role in the positive impact we're making.

I'm thrilled to continue helping you build an unshakeable core to with-stand life's toughest tests, discover the power of pausing before you act, and achieve lasting well-being. The strategies and insights that await you in the pages ahead are truly transformative.

A heartfelt thank you for being part of our journey. Let's keep making a difference, together.

- With gratitude, CalmLogicPress

P.S. - Sharing knowledge is one of the most valuable gifts we can offer. If this book has enlightened your path, why not pass it on to light someone else's way?

CHAPTER FOUR

R: ROLL WITH THE PUNCHES

Don't seek for everything to happen as you wish it would, but rather wish that everything happens as it actually will—then your life will flow well. –Epictetus

D id you know that embracing your fate can lead to a more fulfilling life?

This chapter, which in the VIRTUE framework represents the "R" for "roll with the punches," will explain how we can learn to accept destiny and how this aligns with Stoic principles. We will discuss the concept of amor fati and how it encourages us to not just accept but actively cherish everything that happens to us, whether it's good or bad.

What Is Amor Fati?

Amor fati is a Latin phrase that translates to "love of fate." It encourages us to embrace everything that happens, including suffering and loss, with a positive and accepting attitude. The idea behind the term is to not only be resigned to fate but to actively love and find joy in it, viewing every experience, whether perceived as good or bad, as an essential part of the whole of our life. This acceptance leads to greater personal growth and inner peace.

To apply it, we must consider the power of viewing obstacles not as barriers but as opportunities. When we adopt the love of fate as our mindset, we no longer waste energy resisting the inevitable or lamenting over misfortunes. Instead, we channel our energy into deriving meaning and strength from every situation. Embracing this concept means finding beauty and potential in every moment, even when things don't go our way.

It helps us grow and become better people. So, next time something bad happens, we can remember amor fati and see the misfortune as a chance to learn and practice gratitude. It teaches us that embracing our fate is essential for living a virtuous and resilient life. By fully accepting this, we can transform adversity into opportunities for growth. Embracing the unpredictability of life helps us find joy and meaning in the world, showing us that our attitude toward the inevitable greatly influences our experience of it.

Nietzsche

Although amor fati has deep roots in Stoic philosophy, it was later expanded upon by Friedrich Nietzsche.

Nietzsche, a towering figure in philosophy who lived between 1844 and 1900, left an indelible mark on existential and postmodern thought. His works, characterized by a profound critique of traditional morality, religion, and philosophical dogmatism, emphasize the importance of individual will, power, and the "will to power" as the essence of reality. He is perhaps best known for declaring "God is dead," a statement reflecting his belief in the decline of traditional religious authority and its moral implications for society.

He advocated for the re-evaluation of all personal principles, arguing that the moral and philosophical frameworks of his time were inadequate for the cultivation of a flourishing, powerful individual. Among his most influential concepts is the *Übermensch* or "overman," an ideal for humanity that transcends conventional morality to create new values.

Nietzsche's ideas on eternal recurrence and amor fati further challenge individuals to love and embrace life in its entirety, including its suffering, without resignation but with a vigorous affirmation of existence. His work, though controversial and often misinterpreted, continues to resonate, encouraging a fearless confrontation with the complexities of life and the creation of meaning in an indifferent universe.

The Philosophical Journey of Amor Fati

In exploring the thought surrounding amor fati, we find a fascinating dialogue between Stoicism and Nietzsche's reflections. The latter presents a nuanced critique of Stoicism, particularly targeting its emphasis on rational self-sufficiency and its undervaluation of pain and passion. Nietzsche argues for a profound acceptance of fate that values suffering and pain as essential elements of personal growth and self-mastery, thus enriching the concept of love of fate. This embrace of life's inherent chaos and suffering, according to the German philosopher, is not because they serve a grander purpose but because they are indispensable to the journey toward personal greatness and self-overcoming (Mollison, 2018).

Further examination reveals Nietzsche's notion of amor fati as a pathway to us becoming well-disposed to life and ourselves, a perspective that avoids the problematic implications typically associated with this concept (Brodsky, 1998). This interpretation illuminates a practical approach to embracing the inevitable, suggesting that love, in its ability to see and make things beautiful, plays a crucial role in reconciling with fate's inherent negativity. Such a stance enables us to adopt a positive, affirmative attitude toward our fate, integrating love into the fabric of our existence in a way that transcends mere acceptance.

The concept of amor fati also emerges as an exercise through which we learn to view all aspects of life, including its challenges and adversities, as opportunities for growth and beautification. This practice is not only a theoretical stance but also a way of living that encourages a positive, affirmative response to fate, demonstrating how love can overcome and find value in life's inherent challenges (Elgat, 2016).

Lastly, in times of crisis, Stoicism re-emerges as a belief system capable of fostering existential resilience (Shevchuk, 2023). By advocating for acceptance and the pursuit of virtue regardless of external conditions, the philosophy offers a timeless framework for developing a resilient, flourishing life amid modern existential challenges. It underscores the importance of amor fati in cultivating an attitude of fortitude, growth, and inner peace, transforming obstacles into opportunities for personal development and fulfillment.

The Stoics on Loving Your Fate

The concept of amor fati, particularly in its relationship with free will, presents a nuanced view of how we navigate the complexities of life. On one hand, embracing our fate as dictated by circumstances beyond our control might seem to undermine the concept of freedom of choice.

However, the true essence of cherishing destiny lies not in the denial of unimpeded action but in the harmonious integration of acceptance and agency.

Free will, in this context, is about how we respond to the events of our lives. While we may not have control over what happens to us, we retain the power to choose our reactions. Amor fati encourages us to use our agency to adopt a positive and proactive stance toward life's unpredictabilities. It's about recognizing that while we can't control external events, we do have the autonomy to control our perceptions, emotions, and actions in response to them.

This perspective aligns closely with the Stoic understanding of free will. The ancient philosophy teaches that true freedom lies in our internal state, in our ability to maintain equanimity and make choices aligned with virtue, regardless of external circumstances. The Stoics argue that we can make the best out of any situation. This is where free will asserts itself—not in altering the course of events, but in choosing how to interpret and engage with them.

In Stoicism, the acceptance of everything that happens as part of a rational and purposeful cosmos is central. This recognition is underpinned by a belief in divine providence, suggesting that all events serve a greater purpose within the universe.

Stoic figures like Marcus Aurelius and Epictetus advocated for embracing life's events as necessary components of a predestined plan. Aurelius highlights the importance of aligning our will with the universal order in viewing obstacles as essential for personal growth and the fulfillment of the cosmos' rational structure. Epictetus, meanwhile, emphasizes the importance of distinguishing between what is and isn't within our control, advocating for a peaceful acceptance of external events as part of a divine scheme (*Stoics Believe That Everything That Happens Is Perfect*, 2020).

Friedrich Nietzsche, inspired by Stoic philosophy, offered a different take with his interpretation of amor fati. Nietzsche's thought moves away from the idea of a rational, purposeful universe and instead embraces the inherent chaos and lack of intrinsic meaning in existence. His version of the concept is a passionate acceptance of life's randomness and suffering.

Learning to Embrace Your Destiny

Finding love for your fate is a powerful way to navigate through life with grace and resilience. By accepting and embracing every moment, challenge, and opportunity with enthusiasm, you can change your perspective and find happiness in the ups and downs of life.

Here are some simple ways to incorporate amor fati into your daily life, along with examples to help you understand this empowering philosophy.

- **Embrace the present:** Focus on living in the moment, appreciating life as it unfolds. An example would be someone who takes a moment to notice the beauty in their surroundings during a stressful day, finding calm and appreciation amid chaos.

- **Reflect on mortality:** Use awareness of life's impermanence to deepen your appreciation for the now. In your recognition of the preciousness of each moment, this might involve prioritizing quality time with loved ones over work.

- **Adjust your perceptions:** Challenge and change how you perceive difficult situations, looking for the positive in them. For instance, the next time you have a delayed flight, you can view it as an opportunity to enjoy some reading or engage in conversations with fellow passengers.

- **Learn from obstacles:** View every challenge as an opportunity to grow and learn. Consider the person who sees a job loss as a chance to explore new career possibilities and develop new skills as an example of this.

- **Practice mindfulness:** Cultivate awareness of your thoughts and feelings without making assessments of them, perhaps by dedicating a few minutes each day to meditation, focusing on your breath to bring about a sense of peace.

- **Cultivate positivity:** Focus on maintaining a positive attitude toward life's events, such as making it your practice to start each day by listing three things you're grateful for. This shifts focus from what's lacking to what's abundant.

- **Self-reflection:** Regularly assess how you're applying amor fati in your life by setting aside time to reflect on your progress and areas for improvement, ensuring a continuous journey toward embracing your fate. (Kristenson, 2022; MacRae, 2023; Roy, 2021)

Seeing the Brighter Side of Life

The philosophy of amor fati is a nuanced approach that goes beyond the superficial cheer of "just think positive." It acknowledges the reality of our struggles and the inevitable challenges that life throws our way. Instead of offering a blanket solution to simply ignore the negative or look away from discomfort, it invites us to accept and love our fate, including the painful, difficult, and unexpected parts.

This perspective doesn't trivialize our experiences by suggesting we plaster a smile over our hardships. Rather, it encourages deep, meaningful engagement with life and finding value and purpose in every moment, no matter how hard. By integrating this mindset, we do not dismiss darkness but learn to see the light more clearly, recognizing that growth often requires going through—not skirting around—the obstacles in our path.

Throughout life's journey, we will often face moments that challenge our resilience and optimism. The concept of embracing fate does not glorify suffering such as illness or loss but encourages us to embrace life in its full complexity, with all its ups and downs. By fostering a positive mindset, practicing gratitude, responding with kindness, and seeking learning opportunities in every challenge, we can transform our outlook. We can recognize the silver lining not by overlooking the cloud, but by understanding its role in the broader landscape of our existence.

Adopting amor fati goes beyond merely finding happiness in adversity; it's about developing a profound appreciation for life, despite its inevitable challenges. This perspective invites us to embrace the entire range of human experiences, acknowledging that hardships can pave the way to personal growth and resilience. It reminds us that life's joy doesn't come from avoiding misfortune but from our capacity to remain hopeful, find meaning, and rejoice in the journey, despite its fluctuations. Love of fate is a mindset that equips us to handle difficult times with elegance and discover satisfaction and strength in the act of fully experiencing life, no matter the situation.

Here are some specific examples of situations that can be reframed in a more positive way:

- In dealing with illness, recognize it as a tough yet valuable period for contemplating life's true priorities, deepening relationships, and valuing moments of good health even more.

- Experiencing a breakup, though painful, can be a catalyst for personal development, self-exploration, and a deeper understanding of what you seek in a partner.

- Navigating financial difficulties can enlighten you on budget management and the importance of frugality, and it can motivate you to find innovative ways to cut costs and uncover new sources of income.

Practical Reframing Strategies

The ability to reframe our perspective on challenging situations can significantly influence our overall well-being and happiness. This skill empowers us to find contentment and beauty in our lives, regardless of circumstances. Victor Frankl, in his book *Man's Search for Meaning* (1946), illustrates how even in the direst circumstances, people can find purpose and meaning. His views emphasize the human capacity to transcend suffering and find significance in life's challenges.

Here are some strategies for adjusting your mindset that recognize the transformative power of perspective. They can be applied to a wide variety of situations, and you can also include your actions or reflections on them in your journaling practice:

The 24-Hour Rule

Implement a personal rule where you allow yourself 24 hours to fully experience and dwell on the emotions brought on by a disappointment or setback. After this period, make a conscious effort to find at least one positive takeaway or learning opportunity from the situation. This approach acknowledges your feelings while guiding you toward growth and resilience.

The One-Week Reframing Challenge

Embark on a one-week challenge where you commit to reframing every negative thought into a positive one. Write down these thoughts and their reframed counterparts each day. At the end of the week, review your notes to appreciate how much your perspective has shifted toward positivity and resilience.

Role Model Reflection

Consider someone you admire for their ability to maintain a positive outlook even in tough times. Reflect on how this person might view your current challenges. Imagining their perspective can inspire you to adopt a more positive and constructive approach to your own experiences.

Acts of Kindness

Make it your mission to perform at least one random act of kindness every day. This could be anything from complimenting someone, offering your seat to someone in need, or sending a supportive message to a friend. Observing the positive impact your actions have on others can help shift your focus from personal struggles to the joy of making a difference.

Positive Affirmations

Begin each day with positive affirmations that reinforce your ability to see the good in every situation. Phrases like "Today, I choose to find joy and lessons in all my experiences" can empower you to approach your day with optimism and resilience. This practice sets a positive tone, helping you to navigate life's ups and downs with a grateful heart.

Interactive Element

Gratitude Exercise

Embracing gratitude aligns perfectly with the Stoic principle of amor fati, which invites you to welcome and appreciate life in all its complexity. Stoicism guides you to concentrate on what's within your power and release what isn't. Through gratitude, you learn to see the value in every circumstance. You embody a profound love for your fate by accepting and cherishing all of life's events as integral to the broader tapestry of existence.

By combining the wisdom of Stoicism with gratitude exercises, you can develop a mindset that is strong and appreciative. By doing this, you can practice valuing every moment as an essential part of your life's journey. These examples provide a blueprint for integrating gratitude into your daily life. They demonstrate how small, thoughtful actions can cultivate a deeper sense of appreciation and happiness.

- **Start a gratitude journal:** Each night, write down three things you were grateful for that day, such as a delicious meal, a productive meeting, or a beautiful sunset.

- **Express gratitude to others:** Send a thank-you note or message to a colleague who helped you with a project or to a friend who listened when you needed to talk.

- **Do mindful reflection:** Spend 5 minutes in a quiet space, focusing on a recent event you're thankful for and immersing yourself in the feelings it evokes.

- **Practice gratitude meditation or prayer:** Incorporate phrases of thanks into your meditation or prayer that focus on the blessings in your life.

- **Savor walks:** Take a leisurely walk in a park or your neighborhood, consciously noticing and appreciating the beauty around you—the colors, sounds, and smells.

- **Eat mindfully:** Before eating, take a moment to think about the origin of your food and express thanks for the nourishment it provides.

- **Reframe challenges:** After facing a setback, identify what it taught you or how it made you stronger, focusing on the positive aspects of the challenge.

- **Share gratitude practices:** During dinner with family, take turns sharing one thing you were grateful for that day.

- **Plan for gratitude:** Set a daily alarm as a reminder to pause and think of something you're grateful for, making it a routine part of your day.

- **Persist with practice:** Even on days when finding gratitude feels difficult, jot down the simplest things, like having a roof over your head or the comfort of a warm bed, to maintain a habit of being grateful.

Embracing Life With Amor Fati: Journal Prompts for Self-Acceptance

These journal prompts will help guide you in reflective activities that will allow you to better understand self-acceptance and the importance of embracing the events in your life, fostering a harmonious blend of gratitude for what comes your way and a drive for personal growth.

- **Reflect on a recent challenge:** How did this challenge contribute to your growth, and how can you embrace this experience with love and gratitude as part of your life's journey?

- **Appreciating the journey:** Consider a long-term goal or dream you're working toward. Reflect on the progress you've made rather than the distance you still have to go. How does acknowledging each step forward enrich your appreciation for your journey?

- **Self-acceptance reflection:** Identify a trait you struggle to accept about yourself. How can viewing it through the lens of amor fati change your perspective on its value in your life?

- **The silver linings:** Think about a situation that didn't go as planned. What did you learn from it, and how can you find gratitude in the outcome?

- **Embracing the present:** Describe a moment from today that you would typically overlook. How does paying attention to it and accepting it as it is enrich your experience of life?

Applying Stoic Wisdom

Charles R. Swindoll's quote, "Life is 10% what happens to us and 90% how we react to it" exemplifies the lessons of this chapter. This modern reflection on ancient wisdom is surprisingly adaptable to our modern lives, offering a pathway not only to resolve conflicts but to grow from them.

This perspective can be applied in a practical context, such as when you find yourself entangled in a misunderstanding with a family member. For example, a disagreement with your sister presents an opportunity to practice the Stoic principle of loving your fate.

In the past, such a disagreement might have led to a cycle of blame and regret. You may have replayed the argument over and over in your mind, wishing you had said something differently or that she had been more understanding. Focusing your energy on wishing things were different would be a departure from Stoic philosophy. It locks you into a negative mindset, preventing you from seeing the situation as anything other than a source of frustration and bitterness.

However, by making a few small changes in how you perceive and react to disagreements, you can shift your entire mindset. Instead of dwelling on the argument and wishing it hadn't happened, you can begin to see it as a natural part of your relationship's evolution. This doesn't mean you're happy about it, but you accept it as an opportunity to learn and grow. You start to reflect on your role in the misunderstanding and consider how you might express yourself more clearly in the future. Rather than focusing on placing blame, you focus on understanding and improving the dynamic between you and your sister.

Reaching out to your sibling to discuss the disagreement then becomes an act of amor fati, embodying a love for what life has thrown your way and using it as a chance to deepen your relationship. This proactive step is a significant departure from a pre-Stoic mindset, where you might have waited stubbornly for her to make the first move, or worse, let the rift widen.

The journey toward reconciliation, guided by this principle, transforms the process into something meaningful. It becomes less about resolving the disagreement and more about finding joy and appreciation in the effort to understand each other better.

Conclusion

By exploring the philosophy of accepting our fate, we have learned that amor fati is not about passively resigning ourselves but actively and joyfully embracing all aspects of life. We have seen that it teaches us to gracefully and courageously navigate ups and downs, finding meaning and fulfillment in every moment.

While the Stoics and Nietzsche may have had different perspectives, they both agreed that embracing our fate, whether it brings joy or sorrow, success or failure, is essential for a satisfying and contented life. As we continue growing, this acceptance empowers us to navigate the unpredictable nature of life, using every experience as an opportunity for self-discovery and resilience.

Now, our attention turns from embracing life's inherent unpredictability to building fortitude in the face of its unavoidable challenges. What can we learn from ancient Stoic wisdom about being resilient today? Principles like focusing on what we can control, accepting what we can't change, and maintaining a mindset of calmness in challenging situations help us develop the determination necessary to navigate modern life confidently and gracefully.

CHAPTER FIVE

T: TURN OBSTACLES INTO OPPORTUNITIES

The impediment to action advances action. What stands in the way becomes the way. –Marcus Aurelius

T his quote speaks directly to the subject of this chapter, which represents the "T" for "turning obstacles into opportunities," in the VIRTUE framework. Marcus Aurelius's words illustrate how we can handle tough times in alignment with Stoic lessons. Rather than seeing roadblocks as impossible to overcome, Stoicism teaches us to look at them as chances to grow stronger, keep pushing, and get creative. The quote suggests that the very challenges we face can become pathways that lead to our strengthened character and the advancement of our goals. In other words, impediments to action can actually propel us forward, so what stands in our way becomes our path forward.

The Stoics on Resilience

As we discovered in Chapter 2, Stoicism teaches us to differentiate between the things we can control and the things that are beyond our influence. This means that it encourages us to maintain a sense of calmness and balance in the face of life's unpredictable outcomes.

It urges us to focus on our actions and reactions, which allows us to cultivate a resilient core that remains unaffected by the ups and downs of life.

It is important to note that this indifference isn't a form of apathy but rather a means of safeguarding our emotional well-being. By approaching challenges with reason rather than being driven solely by fleeting emotions, we can both build resilience and also view obstacles as opportunities for personal growth.

For Stoics, resilience is the ability to endure and adapt to adversity through an understanding of what is within our control. It involves accepting external events while maintaining inner tranquility and purposeful action. Related to this, mental toughness involves maintaining a rational and balanced mindset in the face of challenges without allowing external circumstances to disturb our inner peace. It requires persisting with wisdom and ethical integrity, regardless of external pressures. Failure, meanwhile, is not seen as a negative outcome but as an opportunity for learning and growth. It's a chance to practice virtues like courage and wisdom, with a focus on improving our control over our reactions and decisions.

Seneca on Conquering the Conqueror

Seneca, in "On Conquering the Conqueror," delves into the essence of resilience, especially in the face of inevitable death. He illustrates this through the character of Aufidius Bassus, a man whose physical health is failing but whose spirit remains unbroken due to his philosophical outlook.

Seneca argues that philosophy equips us with the ability to face death with joy, strength, and bravery, regardless of our physical condition.

He emphasizes the importance of embracing death as a natural part of life, advocating for a perspective that sees the end of our life as an event that is both inevitable and natural, not as something to be feared. This mindset fosters a form of resilience that allows us to live fully until the very end and to meet death with tranquility and courage rather than fear or despair.

Seneca on Facing Hardships

In "Letter 96" of his *Moral Letters to Lucilius*, Seneca underscores the inevitability of hardships, encouraging a perspective shift toward accepting and anticipating challenges as part of life's natural course. He analogizes life's difficulties to a "tax" that comes with seeking a long life, achievements, and comforts. His wisdom teaches us to expect and embrace challenges rather than being surprised or overwhelmed by them. He advocates for resilience and understanding as the keys to navigating the inevitable (Cullum, 2021).

Historical Examples of Stoicism in Action

These historical examples not only illustrate the application of Stoic philosophy under extreme conditions but also offer profound lessons on the power of resilience, the importance of adhering to our principles, and the distinction between what we can change and what we must accept. They serve as timeless reminders that, while we may not control events, we can always control our responses to them and turn obstacles into opportunities for growth and virtue.

Marcus

Aurelius's Leadership During the Antonine Plague

Marcus Aurelius was also a Roman Emperor who led his empire through one of its most challenging periods—the Antonine Plague. This epidemic, which struck the Roman Empire in 165 C.E., claimed the lives of millions, destabilizing the economy, the military, and the social fabric of Roman society. Amid this chaos, Aurelius remained a paragon of Stoic virtue. His *Meditations*, the thoughts he penned during his military campaigns, reflect his efforts to maintain his composure, rationality, and focus on duty amid despair.

Aurelius viewed the plague not as a personal affront or a disaster to be lamented over but as an obstacle to be navigated with wisdom and courage. His leadership during this time—marked by efforts to provide aid to the afflicted, maintain the stability of the empire, and ensure the continuity of government—demonstrates the Stoic belief in focusing on our responsibilities and what we can control, even in the face of overwhelming crises.

Cato's Opposition to Julius Caesar

Cato the Younger was a staunch defender of the Roman Republic's principles and a vocal critic of Julius Caesar's rise to power. His life embodied the Stoic virtues of integrity, bravery, and commitment to the common good over personal gain. Cato's unwavering stand against the erosion of the Republic's democratic principles, despite the popularity and power of Caesar, showcases the Stoic resolve to uphold our principles even in the face of inevitable defeat.

Cato's suicide, after defeat at the Battle of Thapsus (46 B.C.E.), was his final act of defiance. He chose death over living under tyranny, which is a testament to his belief in freedom and virtue over life itself. His story illustrates the Stoic principle that some things—such as our values and integrity—are worth more than mere survival.

Seneca Advising Nero

Seneca the Younger, a philosopher, playwright, and advisor to Emperor Nero, found himself in a precarious position, navigating the volatile whims of a ruler who gradually descended into tyranny and madness. Seneca attempted to guide his ruler toward wisdom and moderation, embodying the Stoic ideal of remaining steadfast and virtuous even in the most challenging circumstances.

However, as Nero's actions became increasingly cruel and erratic, Seneca's position became untenable. His eventual forced suicide was an order he met with a calm acceptance that reflected his Stoic beliefs. His life and death highlight the complexities of applying Stoic principles in real-world governance and the limits of control we have over others, emphasizing the importance of maintaining inner tranquility and integrity to the end.

Insights From Contemporary Research on Resilience

Research across various fields illuminates the philosophy that obstacles can indeed be transformed into opportunities for growth and fortitude. For example, one study highlights that resilience, defined as successful adaptation to adversity, is crucial for development, especially in children who recover from trauma more effectively when they are supported by stable relationships and personal competencies (Masten et al., 1990).

Another study conducted by Wu et al. (2013) extends this understanding by identifying resilience as an individual's ability to adapt successfully in the face of stress and adversity. Their findings emphasize the role of genetic, developmental, and psychosocial factors in overcoming challenges.

Additional studies such as those of Yeager and Dweck (2012) underscore the significance of growth mindsets in fostering resilience among students who face academic and social challenges. Also in the academic context, advocates have argued for resilience training in nursing education, the purpose of which is to better prepare students for professional challenges. This is noteworthy and underscores the importance of being able to recover from setbacks (Thomas & Asselin, 2018).

Further research contributes to the conceptualization of resilience as a dynamic interaction of psychological characteristics within the stress response process and emphasizes the importance of adaptive processes (Fletcher & Sarkar, 2013). Related to this, the distinction Tan (2013) draws between resilience and post-traumatic recovery underscores the capacity for positive transformation following adversity, reinforcing that we have the potential for growth.

Together, these studies reinforce the Stoic view that facing challenges with determination and a growth mindset can lead to personal betterment and enhanced adaptability.

How to Be Unbreakable

Becoming unbreakable in a Stoic sense means actively applying the philosophy's wisdom to transforming your mindset and forging a character that remains steadfast in the face of adversity. It's about leveraging your understanding of these ancient teachings to foster a mindset that not only endures but thrives on the trials that life presents. This endeavor requires a commitment to practice, reflection, and the consistent application of the four virtues—wisdom, courage, justice, and temperance—in every aspect of life, from the mundane to the profound.

Now that you are familiar with Stoicism, the focus shifts from acquiring knowledge to deepening your practice of the philosophy's teachings. It's about moving beyond the theoretical understanding of concepts like the dichotomy of control, amor fati, and eudaemonia, to embedding these concepts into the fabric of your daily existence. The path to becoming unbreakable, then, is one of continual self-improvement and applying Stoic principles. It involves a deliberate effort to:

- **Control your perceptions:** Recognize that your reaction to any situation is within your control, even if the situation itself is not. Learning to determine how you perceive events is key to maintaining emotional stability and resilience.

- **Embrace obstacles as opportunities:** View every challenge as a chance to grow and strengthen your character. This shift in perspective can significantly improve your resilience by turning adversities into valuable lessons.

- **Practice mindfulness and reflection:** Regularly engage in self-examination like journaling to gain a deeper understanding of your thoughts, emotions, and behaviors. This can help you remain present and make more deliberate decisions aligned with your values.

- **Develop an attitude of gratitude:** Focus on being thankful for what you have rather than dwelling on what you lack. Use the gratitude exercise from the last chapter as a starting point. You will see that gratitude fosters a positive outlook and helps maintain mental fortitude in tough times.

- **Use cognitive behavioral techniques:** Recognize and challenge negative thoughts to reshape your perceptions and reactions. This practice is rooted in both Stoicism and CBT, emphasizing the power of thought in influencing feelings and behaviors.

- **Set clear, achievable goals:** Break down larger goals into smaller, manageable tasks. This strategy not only makes your objectives more attainable but also helps maintain motivation and willpower by providing clear direction and immediate feedback.

- **Cultivate a support network:** Build and maintain relationships with individuals who support your growth and share your values. A strong community can provide encouragement, advice, and different perspectives when you face challenges. (MacRae, 2021; Hughes, 2017; Robertson, 2022)

Picking Yourself Back Up Again

Failing is as certain as day turning into night, and it will shape your path in unexpected ways. Acknowledging and analyzing failures goes beyond just acceptance. You need to thoroughly examine the missteps and misunderstandings that led to your setback without allowing them to overshadow your entire identity.

Stoics take responsibility for their role in any setback. This is a process of reflection that encourages us to confront the actions that precipitated failure, enabling us to distill valuable lessons that can avert similar pitfalls as we move forward. Embracing our feelings plays a pivotal role in this journey, as we need to allow ourselves to experience disappointment or sadness without becoming ensnared by them. This kind of emotional attunement paves the way for using these sentiments as catalysts for motivation and change.

Overcoming obstacles requires challenging our irrational beliefs about setbacks. This involves shifting from negative, self-defeating thoughts to a mindset that is more balanced and constructive. For instance, swapping "I'll never succeed" with "I can learn and try a different approach next time" is a significant step forward. Crafting a realistic plan is an integral part of this process. By setting achievable goals based on our experiences, we prepare for future endeavors rooted in the lessons we have learned.

When Things Go Wrong

Contemplating and assessing setbacks in your Stoic journaling routine can help you transform failure into a stepping stone toward your enhanced personal and professional development. This is in harmony with the Stoic quest for virtue and self-improvement, and routine reflection prompts you to constantly extract insights from your experiences. Start by answering these questions:

- What can I learn from this experience?

- Were there any assumptions I had that led me to this outcome?

- How can I improve my approach or strategy?

- Did I fully commit to my goals, or were there areas of hesitation?

- What alternative actions could I have taken?

- Is there a skill or knowledge gap that I need to address?

- Who can I seek guidance from to gain a better perspective?

- How can I better manage risks in the future?

- Was the timing right for my actions?

- How effective was my communication with others involved?

- In what ways can I strengthen my resilience and capacity to rebound?

- What positives can I extract from this situation?

- How will I adjust my plans to incorporate these lessons?

- What steps can I take to ensure better preparation for future endeavors?

Developing a No-Fail Mindset

As Epictetus stated, "It's not what happens to you but how you react to it that matters," emphasizing the importance of our attitude toward challenges (*Stress Management*, n.d.). Stoics see obstacles as opportunities to practice virtues such as courage and perseverance. The fusion of ancient Stoic wisdom with modern psychological principles reveals a profound similarity: Both share the belief that how we respond to challenges shapes our personal growth. Just as Stoics saw obstacles as opportunities to develop virtues, the growth mindset regards difficulties as crucial for learning and progress.

A growth mindset, as conceptualized by Carol Dweck, is the belief that abilities and intelligence can be developed through dedication, hard work, and embracement of challenges. It contrasts with a fixed mindset, where abilities are perceived as static and unchangeable. Those with a growth mindset don't perceive failures as evidence of intrinsic shortcomings but react to them as springboards for developing and stretching their existing abilities.

Growth vs. Fixed Mindset

Stoicism encourages embracing what life throws at us with composure and resilience, much like the growth mindset approaches challenges and obstacles. The comparison between the two mindsets highlights a fundamental difference in how individuals approach learning and failure. While those with a fixed mindset avoid challenges, give up easily, and see effort as fruitless because they accept talents to be innate, people with a growth mindset embrace challenges, persist through obstacles, learn from criticism, and see effort as a path to mastery.

Advantages of a Growth Mindset

The following quote by Seneca speaks to the Stoic attitude to a growth mindset: "I judge you unfortunate because you have never lived through misfortune. You have passed through life without an opponent—no one can ever know what you are capable of, not even you."

Having a growth mindset offers numerous advantages, including en-hanced learning and resilience. It fosters a passion for knowledge rather than a hunger for approval, encourages resilience in the face of setbacks, and facilitates a more open and optimistic approach to personal and professional challenges, leading to higher achievement and greater satisfaction in life.

- **Enhanced learning:** A growth mindset fosters a continuous desire for knowledge and skill development while also en-couraging curiosity and exploration, leading to deeper under-standing and innovation.

- **Increased resilience:** It builds the fortitude to bounce back from failures and setbacks. The growth mindset also cultivates the ability to persevere through challenges and view them as opportunities for development.

- **Passion for learning over approval:** This mindset prioritizes personal development and mastery of topics over seeking ex-ternal validation. By adopting it, you can reduce your fear of failure, as the focus shifts from being judged to learning and improving.

- **Encouragement of resilience in setbacks:** Prioritizing growth teaches that setbacks are part of the learning process and not indicators of inability. It helps in maintaining motiva-tion and commitment in the face of difficulties.

- **An open and optimistic approach to challenges:** The posi-tive outlook on new challenges that the growth mindset pro-motes helps you see them as chances to extend your abili-ties. This can also facilitate creativity and flexibility in problem-solving.

- **Higher achievement and satisfaction:** This way of thinking leads to setting higher goals and making more significant efforts to achieve them. The result is a sense of fulfillment from overcoming obstacles and making progress.

- **Improved adaptability:** The flexibility to change that a growth mentality encourages is crucial in both personal growth and professional environments. You can thereby enhance your ability to navigate uncertainty and adapt strategies as needed.

- **Greater collaboration and communication:** The mindset promotes an environment of mutual learning and support among you and your peers. It enhances your listening and feedback skills, which are vital for effective teamwork and leadership.

- **Increased grit and determination:** You can develop grit, a powerful predictor of success, through consistent effort and dedication to growth. You can also foster a long-term commitment to your goals despite the challenges and setbacks you may experience.

- **Development of empathy and self-compassion:** The growth mindset encourages understanding and compassion toward yourself and others during the learning process. It also leads to a more supportive and encouraging community, both personally and professionally.

How to Cultivate a Growth Mindset

Cultivating a growth mindset involves recognizing and adjusting your thought patterns and attitudes toward learning and failure. The following are all excellent strategies to incorporate:

- **Embracing challenges:** Actively seek out new challenges and view them as opportunities to grow rather than threats to avoid. This involves stepping out of your comfort zone and engaging in tasks that test your abilities. The approach is similar to the Stoic practice of voluntary discomfort, which helps develop resilience and adaptability.

- **Persisting in the face of setbacks:** Develop resilience by maintaining focus and motivation even when you are faced with difficulties. You can do this by understanding that setbacks are not failures but part of the learning journey, emphasizing the Stoic value of enduring hardship with a calm mind.

- **Seeing effort as a path to mastery:** Recognize that effort is a crucial ingredient for success and mastery. It's not just about innate talent but about the consistent work put into improving and learning. Remember that Stoic philosophy encourages embracing challenges and exerting effort as the means to develop virtue and excellence in character.

- **Learning from criticism:** Approach criticism with an open mind, in accordance with Stoic principles. See it as valuable feedback that can inform your growth and development. Instead of taking it personally, use it constructively to make adjustments and improvements. Detach yourself from your ego and value critique as a tool for self-improvement.

- **Finding lessons and inspiration in the success of others:** Look to the achievements of others not as a source of envy but as motivation and evidence of what's possible. Learn from their journeys, strategies, and setbacks to enrich your own path to growth. Stoic philosophers learned from others who were wise and successful, seeing their examples as a guide to forging their own path to virtue.

Growth Mindset Tips

Integrating these growth mindset tips into your daily thinking brings about small but powerful shifts:

- Set learning goals instead of performance goals.

- Place greater value on the process than the end result.

- Use constructive criticism as feedback for growth.

- Surround yourself with others who embody a growth mindset.

- Celebrate effort and progress, not just material success.

Interactive Element

Visualizing the Negative

Imagine facing the toughest moments of your life—loss, failure, or any other setback. Now, picture these events not with fear but with a calm mind and readiness to embrace whatever comes your way. This is the essence of negative visualization, a Stoic practice that teaches you to prepare mentally for life's challenges. By contemplating these scenarios, you learn to value your present more deeply and understand that hardships are not just obstacles but opportunities for growth and resilience.

Start small by incorporating this exercise into your daily routine, and as you do, remember: It's about finding balance. It's not about dwelling in pessimism but about empowering yourself to face life with courage and appreciation.

1. Take a moment to contemplate potential losses or challenges you might face. Consider losing everything, from your personal treasures like your home, car, and keepsakes to your social world, including family, friends, and pets. Reflect on what it would be like to no longer have the elements of your professional life, such as your job and those you work with. Contemplate not having access to your favorite foods, brands, and TV shows, as well as not being able to do hobbies like sports, crafts, and volunteering.

2. Envision the loss of each of these as detailed scenarios, as if they're happening now, not in the future.

3. Remind yourself that these events, should they occur, are opportunities to demonstrate virtue and resilience.

4. Record the experience in your journal and repeat the reflections. Use them to foster a greater appreciation for your current circumstances, reducing your fear of loss or change.

Tips

- **Start with small, manageable scenarios:** Beginning with less daunting situations helps ease you into the practice of negative visualization without overwhelming your emotions. You should aim to build resilience gradually, so you need to ensure that you're not deterred by the intensity of the exercise.

- **Maintain balance to avoid becoming overly pessimistic:** The goal is to prepare not to despair. Keeping a balanced outlook ensures that while you're ready for the worst, you remain hopeful about the future. Keeping the positive in sight prevents the exercise from breeding fear or negativity.

- **Integrate this practice into daily routines:** Making negative visualization a part of your daily life turns it into a habit that naturally strengthens your mental resilience. Regular practice ensures that when challenges do arise, you're well-prepared to face them with calmness and poise.

- **Add your visualizations to your journal:** Writing down your thoughts and feelings during each session can help you track your progress, insights, and emotional growth over time.

Applying Stoic Wisdom

In the aftermath of a breakup, the initial wave of emotions can feel insurmountable. Yet, within this tumult lies an opportunity for profound personal growth and transformation, a sentiment echoed in this quote: "The obstacle in the path becomes the path. Never forget, within every obstacle is an opportunity to improve our condition" (Holiday, 2009).

When you find yourself in a similar scenario, begin by shifting how you perceive the relationship's end. Instead of viewing it as a loss, see it as an opportunity to re-evaluate your life and priorities. This doesn't mean dismissing your feelings but rather allowing them to be a catalyst for positive change. Embrace the Stoic practice of focusing on what you can control—your thoughts, actions, and reactions—while accepting what you cannot change.

Be kind to yourself during this time. Recognize that healing is not linear and that it's okay to have days when you feel less than your best. Incorporate practices such as mindfulness or meditation into your daily routine to foster a sense of calm and centeredness. This act of self-care is a step toward building the resilience that Stoicism speaks of, allowing you to maintain inner tranquility amid external upheaval.

Use journaling as a tool for reflection and self-discovery. Writing about your thoughts and feelings can help you process the breakup and understand your role in the relationship dynamics. This introspection can reveal patterns that may benefit from change, encouraging personal growth and greater emotional intelligence moving forward.

After a breakup, the future may seem daunting. Break down your larger aspirations into smaller, manageable tasks. This could be as simple as dedicating 15 minutes a day to a new hobby or setting a goal to meet with friends once a week. These small victories can boost your confidence and remind you of your capacity to create positive change in your life.

Lean on friends and family for support but also consider joining clubs or groups that align with your interests. Connecting with new people can provide fresh perspectives and opportunities for growth. Remember, building a strong support network is not just about receiving but also about giving support to others and fostering both a sense of community and belonging.

Embrace the philosophy that challenges, including breakups, are opportunities for personal development. Encourage yourself to adopt a growth mindset by viewing this experience as a chance to learn and evolve. This perspective shift is powerful, allowing you to see every obstacle as a stepping stone toward becoming a stronger, more resilient version of yourself.

In moments of hardship, it's easy to lose sight of the positives in our lives, so start or end each day by listing three things you're grateful for. This practice can shift your focus from what you've lost to the abundance that remains, nurturing a positive outlook and resilience in the face of adversity.

Conclusion

Throughout history, obstacles have led to big changes and successes. Facing challenges with courage and persistence helps us grow and move forward. With a shift in mindset, difficulties can be seen not as things that stop us but as chances to learn and get stronger. They help us adjust and improve. By overcoming them, we find out what we can really do, which is often more than we think, and understand ourselves better.

In the next chapter, we will explore the profound impact of releasing—letting go of our wants, freeing ourselves from distractions, and breaking away from harmful connections that clutter our existence. The "U" of the VIRTUE framework, with its emphasis on unburdening, will encourage us to relinquish what burdens us. We can then open up room for clarity, meaning, and satisfaction to blossom. Come along as

we investigate the empowering journey toward a simpler, more purposeful lifestyle.

CHAPTER SIX

U: UNBURDEN YOURSELF FROM THE UNNECESSARY

It is not the man who has too little but the man who craves more that is poor. –Seneca

In the VIRTUE framework, the "u" that stands for "unburdening yourself from the unnecessary" embodies the wisdom of Seneca, who teaches us that true wealth lies not in our possessions but in mastering our desires. These insights remind us that real prosperity is not about what we own but rather about our inner desires.

In this chapter, we will explore ancient Stoic guidance and invite you to discover how adopting a mindset free of ego can lead to genuine happiness, reduced stress, and stronger relationships. We will learn about Stoic perspectives on fame, ego, and the importance of living a life guided by self-control and introspection. We will also reflect on how these views can guide us on how to prioritize what truly matters, find joy in simplicity, and embrace a life of virtue over the fleeting allure of external approval. Furthermore, we will discuss how simplifying both our physical and mental spaces can open the door to a more focused and satisfying life.

The Stoics on Fame and Ego

In Stoic philosophy, as articulated by Marcus Aurelius and Epictetus, the pursuit of fame and glory is deemed a futile endeavor, one that detracts from the essence of a virtuous life. Marcus Aurelius emphasizes the transient nature of fame by stating, "The people who admire you now will soon be dead," highlighting the temporary and ultimately meaningless quest for praise. Similarly, Epictetus advises, "If you wish to be loved by anyone, love yourself," underscoring the importance of self-respect over seeking approval from others (*Stoic Quotes on Fame and Vanity*, n.d.).

Both argue that fame is ephemeral, a fleeting whisper soon forgotten after our demise, and they caution against letting the desire for external validation dictate our actions. For them, true value lies not in us being recognized by others but in our integrity and pursuit of virtue. Stoicism thus invites a reflective inward turn, emphasizing self-contentment and the cultivation of personal ethics, virtues, and integrity over the allure of fame and vanity.

Seneca's Wisdom

Seneca wrote about the foundational ideas of reducing ego, prioritizing internal virtues, and highlighting the importance of simplicity in attaining a fulfilling life. His discussions on the passing nature of celebrity, the futility of seeking status, and the shallowness of mental acrobatics serve as important reflections that emphasize focusing on self-improvement, ethical behavior, and the development of personal virtues instead of accolades and societal approval.

On the Relativity of Fame

The ancient philosopher spoke about how fame and importance depend on the situation (The Stoic, 2021a). He compared this to a ship that seems big in a river but small in the ocean, showing that what matters is where and how we see things. He also suggested that being truly important means being good and honest in front of others and to ourselves. This idea tells us that being virtuous and doing the right thing is more valuable than chasing after glory.

On the Vanity of Place Seeking

Seneca's message in *On the Vanity of Place Seeking* (n.d.) is pretty straightforward: Chasing after high-status jobs or titles just because they seem impressive isn't worth it. He thought that we should spend more time looking inward and figuring out who we are instead of trying to impress others. According to him, being true to ourselves and not getting caught up in the rat race for recognition or power is where real happiness and freedom lie. He argued that true respect and greatness come from how we live our lives, not the titles we hold.

On the Vanity of Mental Gymnastics

Seneca spoke about how some people like to show off by using complicated ideas in philosophy, but that doesn't help them grow as people (*On the Vanity of Mental Gymnastics*, n.d.). He believed that truly engaging with philosophy—the kind that touches the heart and changes people—makes us stronger and better, not just on the outside but deep down. This kind of fundamental change is something that luck can't give or take away. It shows that a person is solid and steady, no matter what ups and downs life throws at them, unlike just playing with fancy words and ideas.

The Egoless Mindset

Stoic philosophy offers a profound pathway for us to liberate ourselves from the shackles of ego, again emphasizing the cultivation of inner virtues and ethical living. At the heart of this transformative journey is the application of Stoicism's core virtues—wisdom, courage, justice, and temperance—in daily life.

By engaging in mindfulness, we gain the ability to observe our thoughts and emotions from a distance, reducing the grip of the ego on our lives. The clarity of mind we gain reveals how conceit shapes our perceptions and actions. Breaking free from it paves the way for a more authentic and virtuous existence.

Practicing Stoicism involves a deliberate shift in focus from seeking external approval to nurturing internal virtues and finding satisfaction within ourselves. This philosophical approach teaches the importance of accepting adversity as a catalyst for personal growth and resilience. Through regular self-reflection, we can uncover and challenge the desires and motivations fueled by ego, promoting a simpler, more purposeful life that is in harmony with nature.

Moreover, the philosophy encourages viewing challenges as opportunities to strengthen our character and advance on the path to personal excellence, free from the need for praise (Davenport, 2022). By prioritizing wisdom, courage, justice, and temperance, as well as inner peace, we can achieve a state of contentment and fulfillment that is not easily disturbed by outside circumstances.

These practices not only aim to diminish the influence of the ego but also foster a deeper sense of connection and compassion toward others. In recognizing the interconnectedness of all beings, Stoicism advocates for a life that values humility, self-awareness, and a focus on what truly matters—living virtuously. By embracing these principles, we can navigate life with a lighter burden of pride, leading to a profound sense of fulfillment.

The Stoics on Ditching the Inessential

In exploring Stoicism's perspective on wealth, we find a belief system deeply relevant to today's society, where materialism often takes center stage. The philosophy does not categorically denounce material prosperity; rather, it suggests that the value and impact of riches depend significantly on how wealth is perceived and used (Weaver, 2022).

Seneca encapsulated this view by suggesting that poverty is not a matter of how little we have but rather how much we desire. He implied that the relentless pursuit of more can lead to a sense of poverty, regardless of our material possessions. This perspective is particularly poignant in a world where consumer culture and advertising constantly push the narrative that happiness is just one purchase away.

Stoicism teaches that wealth itself is neither inherently good nor bad. What matters is our attitude toward it. Material abundance becomes problematic when it distracts or detracts from living a virtuous life. If it is pursued at the expense of others, or if it fosters an attachment that disturbs peace of mind and moral integrity, we should view it negatively. Conversely, if it is a byproduct of our pursuit of virtue, such as the gains from a career aimed at helping others, we can consider it neutral or even positive.

The Stoic approach to wealth is marked by a call for moderation and wisdom. Followers of the philosophy advocate for a balanced lifestyle where possessions are not accumulated excessively but are sufficient for living a comfortable life. They warn against the "hedonic treadmill," a state where the pursuit of more leads to perpetual dissatisfaction. They suggest instead that true contentment comes from appreciating what we already have (Weaver, 2022).

Seneca's Wisdom

On the Philosopher's Mean

Seneca, in his "Letter V. On the Philosopher's Mean," explores finding a balance in life that steers clear of both extremes: living too luxuriously and rejecting societal norms completely (2020c). He suggests aiming for a middle ground—living simply yet not so austerely that it alienates us from society. This approach helps us focus on both personal development and connecting with others around us. Seneca's advice is about blending in externally while nurturing our internal virtues, promoting a life of dignity and moderation.

On Philosophy and Riches

In Seneca's "Letter XVII. On Philosophy and Riches," he shares a crucial insight: True contentment and wisdom aren't found in wealth but through engaging with philosophy (2020d). He advises us to view material possessions with detachment and to use whatever wealth we have ethically and generously. Wisdom, not financial prosperity, is what provides a deeper, more meaningful path to fulfillment. So, if you're looking to enrich your life, Seneca suggests turning to philosophy for treasures that money can't buy.

On True and False Riches

"On True and False Riches" invites us to rethink our priorities, high-lighting the emptiness in the relentless pursuit of wealth and material goods (n.d.). Seneca suggests that true wealth lies in embracing a life of virtue, which brings genuine satisfaction and happiness. According to Seneca, the essence of real richness is found in a contented heart and living in harmony with nature, challenging us to find value in who we are and how we conduct our lives.

The Art of Wanting Less and Practicing Moderation

In the Stoic journey toward self-improvement and contentment, want-ing less and practicing moderation emerge as vital disciplines. These principles challenge us to refine our desires, prioritize character devel-opment over material accumulation, and seek fulfillment from within. Stoicism, by advocating a life aligned with virtue and nature, encour-ages a shift away from the relentless pursuit of external validation. Embracing these ideals fosters gratitude and resilience, and it also en-riches our existence with genuine well-being and growth, steering us toward a life of purpose and balance.

On Wanting Less

In the quest for contentment and mental well-being, reducing our wants can be a transformative practice. The teachings of Stoicism, namely focusing on fewer yearnings, align with modern strategies to cultivate happiness by managing desires. Here are consolidated strategies from various sources on how to achieve this (Bennett, 2021; Tsatiris, 2022):

- **Practice gratitude:** Keeping a gratitude journal to regularly reflect on what you're thankful for can shift your focus from what you're lacking to the abundance present in life, fostering a sense of contentment.

- **Engage in reflection and meditation:** These practices help in acknowledging and appreciating the positives in life, allowing for a deeper understanding of your needs versus wants.

- **Manage expectations and desires:** Actively questioning why you want something can lead to a realization that many desires are superficial and not crucial for happiness. This insight can change your relationship with materialism and reduce the inclination to accumulate unnecessary items.

- **Know where to set the bar:** Cultivating realistic expectations about how achievements will impact your life helps in understanding that the satisfaction from success is often fleeting. This realization encourages focusing on what truly brings you joy rather than chasing after endless goals.

- **Press the brakes:** Taking time to appreciate the present and the small joys in life rather than constantly aiming for the next achievement can lead to a deeper sense of fulfillment and contentment.

On Moderation

To lead a balanced and fulfilling life, Stoic philosophers practice moderation as a core principle. They believe that excess, whether in emotions, physical pleasures, or material possessions, can disturb the tranquility of the mind and hinder our ability to live virtuously. Moderation, therefore, is not about denying ourselves pleasures but about finding the right measure in all aspects of life. This balance is crucial for achieving eudaemonia, a state of contentment and flourishing that comes from living in alignment with reason and virtue.

- **Embrace imperfection:** Accept that perfection is unattainable and that striving for it can lead to excessive behaviors. Embracing flaws can foster moderation by reducing the pressure to exceed limits.

- **Prioritize experiences over possessions:** Shifting focus from acquiring material items to experiencing life can naturally lead to moderation in consumption and foster richer, more fulfilling life experiences.

- **Set boundaries for work and leisure:** Balancing work and relaxation prevents burnout and promotes a moderate approach to both productivity and leisure.

- **Practice mindful eating:** Paying attention to hunger cues and savoring meals slowly can promote a moderate and healthy relationship with food.

- **Digital detox:** Regularly unplugging from technology encourages moderation in screen time, leading to increased mindfulness and presence. (Favreau, n.d.; Samuels, 2017)

The Stoics on Surrounding Yourself With the Right People

Stoic philosophy invites you to view love as a pathway to enhancing your character; it urges you to seek partners who inspire a virtuous life.

Relationships should not just be about emotional or physical connection. They should also be about fostering mutual respect, understanding, and a shared pursuit of the good life. This view encourages rational and selfless love that aligns with living harmoniously with nature and reason (Sadler, 2018).

Embracing Stoic principles in your relationships helps deepen your connections, making them more resilient to external pressures and internal conflicts. It also highlights the importance of self-control, understanding, and adaptability. The philosophy teaches you that, while you can't control others, you can manage your reactions to them, promoting resilience and the ability to face relationship challenges with a calm mind.

Choosing the right company is essential for your personal and ethical growth. Stoicism advises surrounding yourself with people who embody the virtues you admire, as their influence can shape your character. By engaging with those who demonstrate wisdom, courage, justice, and moderation, you're encouraged to cultivate these qualities within yourself, creating a supportive and virtuous environment for your personal development.

Seneca's Wisdom

On True and False Friendships

In "Letter III. On True and False Friendship," Seneca delves into the essence of platonic relationships, emphasizing the crucial role of trust (2020). He advises careful judgment before forming friendships and advocates for a deep understanding of a person's character. He stresses that once a friendship is established, trust should be unwavering. He also warns against the extremes of either trusting everyone or no one, suggesting a balanced approach instead. Ultimately, Seneca's guidance underscores the importance of discernment. He urges us to commit wholeheartedly to those we deem trustworthy and to navigate the delicate balance of trust with wisdom.

On Good Company

Seneca reflects on the value of choosing our company wisely in "On Good Company." He critiques those who claim to be too busy for philosophical study due to numerous engagements, suggesting instead that true engagement comes from within. Seneca cherished his time with true friends and great thinkers of the past. In his reflection on this, he emphasized the importance of internal wealth over external riches. In the letter, he illustrates this through his admiration for Demetrius the Cynic, who lived a life of simplicity and contentment and embodied the Stoic ideal of valuing wisdom over material wealth.

Dealing With Toxic People

When confronted with rudeness or toxicity, Stoicism provides strategies for maintaining our composure. It suggests seeing challenges as opportunities to strengthen virtues such as patience and understanding. By acknowledging that others' actions are beyond our control, we can focus on managing our responses.

The philosophy promotes empathy toward difficult individuals, encouraging us to understand that hurtful behavior is a reflection of the offender's struggles. It urges us to set healthy boundaries to safeguard our well-being while we nurture compassion. So, we should reflect on these interactions as chances for personal growth, recognizing that our reaction—rooted in integrity and resilience—is a testament to our character.

Stoic principles advocate for mastering destructive emotions by practicing indifference, avoiding impulsive reactions, and engaging in thoughtful discourse during disagreements. An instance of this attitude is expressed by Marcus Aurelius, who reflected on the insignificance of getting upset over natural human occurrences, such as body odor, acknowledging they are not intentional offenses (Daily Stoic, 2017).

Stoic thinkers emphasize prioritizing logic over emotion, contemplating shared mortality, avoiding excess and material pursuits, and fulfilling relationship obligations with fairness and kindness. These practices encourage us to view challenges as opportunities to strengthen our virtues and achieve balance. When we implement them, we can foster empathy, establish healthy boundaries, and focus on personal development through integrity and resilience.

Stoics practice the art of not internalizing situations, recognizing that most negative behaviors are not directed toward them. Likewise, encountering individuals who are impolite is an inevitable part of human variability. Instead, Stoics reflect on the true impact of rudeness, questioning the real harm it causes. Epictetus highlighted that hurt is a matter of perception, suggesting that feeling injured is a choice.

Lastly, Stoicism advocates for avoiding reciprocating rudeness and promotes rising above it. Marcus Aurelius urged being better rather than seeking revenge while Seneca emphasized healing over vengeance, noting the latter's potential for causing greater harm.

Interactive Element

Declutter and Reset

Decluttering transcends mere aesthetics: It offers profound benefits that impact our mental health, relationships, and physical well-being. This multifaceted approach to simplifying our lives not only enhances our living spaces but also promotes a deeper sense of mental clarity and emotional balance.

Clearing our spaces plays a significant role in reducing stress and improving focus. The visual chaos of clutter competes for our attention, detracting from our ability to concentrate and complete tasks efficiently. Notably, one study found that women who described their homes using positive language exhibited lower levels of cortisol, the stress hormone, compared to those who perceived their homes as cluttered (WebMD Editorial Contributors, 2021). This suggests that a more organized environment can alleviate stress and foster a sense of calm and control.

Moreover, the physical act of decluttering can have a therapeutic effect, serving as a medium for physical activity that enhances creativity and relaxation. The process of sorting through belongings can also lead to a boost in mood and physical health (Beckwith & Parkhurst, 2021). The satisfaction derived from creating order out of disorder not only reduces stress but also instills a sense of achievement and well-being in us.

Minimizing mess also has the potential to improve our relationships. A tidy home environment can decrease the likelihood of conflict over clutter and make spaces more welcoming for friends and family. This emphasizes how an ordered space can foster better interpersonal dynamics and a more inviting atmosphere for social interactions (Mather Hospital, 2017).

In addition to psychological benefits, clearing away clutter can have tangible effects on our physical health. By removing the dust, mold, and mildew that thrive in cluttered environments, we can lower our risk of asthma and allergies. A clean and orderly space also encourages healthier lifestyle choices, such as cooking and sleeping better, highlighting the interconnectedness of our physical environment and our physical health.

Decluttering can also serve as a catalyst for personal growth and self-reflection. It prompts us to evaluate what possessions truly add value to our lives, helping us to let go of the past and focus on our present and future goals. This process of introspection and letting go can be liberating, offering a path to a more minimalistic and purposeful lifestyle.

The journey of decluttering, therefore, is not just about creating a more aesthetically pleasing space but about fostering a healthier, more focused, and more fulfilling life. The benefits extend beyond the visible, touching on aspects of mental health, personal relationships, and overall well-being, making it a practice worth adopting for anyone seeking to improve their quality of life.

Here are some tips to help you get started:

- **Start small:** Begin your decluttering journey by focusing on a small, manageable area, such as a single drawer or a specific folder on your computer. This approach helps you build momentum for tackling larger spaces.

- **Dedicate time:** Allocate specific months to focus on different categories of clutter in your life, such as clothing, paperwork, or digital files. This systematic approach prevents the process from becoming overwhelming and ensures thoroughness.

- **Stop new acquisitions:** Implement a pause on bringing new items into your home to prevent adding to the clutter. This step is crucial for gaining control over your environment and making mindful choices about what deserves space in your life.

- **Evaluate items:** For every item in your space, ask yourself if it serves a functional purpose or brings you joy. If it does neither, consider it a candidate for donation or disposal, simplifying your surroundings and your life.

- **Celebrate wins:** Take time to acknowledge and celebrate the completion of each milestone, no matter how small. This positive reinforcement encourages continued effort and highlights the progress you've made.

- **Set clear goals:** Establish specific, achievable goals for each clearing session, such as the number of items to sort through or a particular area to organize. Clear objectives help you maintain focus and motivation.

- **Follow a regular schedule:** Designate regular, consistent times in your schedule for decluttering activities. This commitment ensures steady progress and integrates the practice into your routine as a sustainable habit.

- **Reflect on progress:** Periodically review the areas you've organized to appreciate the progress you've made. This reflection helps maintain your momentum and provides an opportunity for you to adjust your strategy as needed.

- **Limit intake:** Before acquiring new items, ensure that they have a clear purpose or bring significant joy into your life. This mindful approach will help you maintain a clutter-free environment and prioritize quality over quantity.

- **Mindful decisions:** Adopt a slow and thoughtful approach to decluttering. Consider the purpose and emotional value of each item. This process ensures that only those items that truly add value remain in your space, leading to a more intentional and fulfilling living environment.

Applying Stoic Wisdom

Facing a disappointing monthly bank statement is a scenario many of us know all too well. Despite putting in the hours, financial stability seems just out of reach, leading to a cycle of stress and frustration. This predicament often stems from a simple yet profound misunderstanding that Seneca highlighted: It's not the lack of possessions but the endless desire for more that leaves us feeling impoverished.

A famous quote by Will Rogers exemplifies the modern attitude to prosperity: "Too many people spend money they haven't earned to buy things they don't want to impress people they don't like." In a society that measures success by material wealth, it's easy to fall into this trap of perpetual spending. However, redefining wealth can offer a way out. Instead, we can think of wealth as something found in the freedom to enjoy life's simplest pleasures, the capacity to share with others, and the peace of mind that comes from financial security.

To achieve this, start by acknowledging what you're grateful for that doesn't cost anything. This approach can lead to more thoughtful spending on things that genuinely matter. Examining your financial habits to distinguish between wants and needs can also reduce unnecessary expenses. Similarly, embracing a simpler lifestyle often results in greater happiness than a life cluttered with possessions. Opting for experiences over tangible goods can lead to lasting joy, and a pause before purchasing can prevent regretting impulse buys.

Establishing an emergency fund is a smart move for financial stability and improving your financial knowledge leads to smarter choices. When you're dealing with financial pressures, it's crucial to understand that your worth isn't tied to your bank balance. Adopting practices like reflecting on what you're thankful for and focusing on aspects of your life that you can control can fundamentally change your outlook from one of lack to one of sufficiency.

The essence of financial well-being lies in wanting less and being satisfied with simplicity. Adopting this mindset not only aids in better financial management but also contributes to a more fulfilling life. It encourages a shift in perspective from incessantly seeking more to valuing what you already have, thereby alleviating financial worries and enhancing your overall life quality.

Conclusion

This chapter has been about minimizing ego and prioritizing internal virtues over seeking external approval and guiding you toward releasing material desires, distractions, and unhealthy connections. It's been about clearing your life and mind for a more purposeful existence, drawing on Stoic views on fame and ego. It has also introduced you to Seneca's wisdom on fame's relativity, insights that advocate for simplicity and introspection. The chapter showed you that by decluttering both physically and mentally, you can learn to live with intention, enhance your relationships, and achieve personal growth.

Next, in the following chapter titled "Embrace the Ephemeral Nature of Existence," marking the "E" of the VIRTUE framework, we'll embrace life's fleeting nature. By acknowledging this transience, you will learn to view each day as a chance to improve yourself and deepen your connections, fostering gratitude for the present and life's beauty.

Chapter Seven

E: Embrace the Ephemeral Nature of Existence

Have you ever teetered on the edge of existence, where life and death blurred into one?

Do you know what it's like to face your final hours?

In 2006, Anita Moorjani found out.

While she was battling terminal cancer, she slipped into a coma only to experience a near-death revelation that not only brought her back from the brink but also miraculously healed her. Her encounter with the beyond transformed her, instilling an intense gratitude for life and a profound understanding of her purpose.

For those who haven't experienced an event of this intensity, consider something more mundane yet just as revealing. Think of how frustrated you feel when the water supply in your home is shut off unexpectedly, or a power outage plunges your world into darkness. Suddenly, the things you take for granted become the center of your universe.

Or on an even more relatable note, remember how you longed to breathe freely through both nostrils while in the throes of a persistent cold?

These examples serve as an introduction to this final chapter of the VIRTUE framework in which we address the "E" that encourages you to embrace the ephemeral and accept life's impermanence. They are all reminders that it's normal not to appreciate some things until they're out of reach, even if only momentarily, and so it is with life.

You might find yourself steering clear of thoughts about death, and you're not alone in this. This avoidance springs from a cocktail of psychological discomfort, societal taboos, deep-seated existential worries, and even your evolutionary wiring. The fear and uncertainty that dying brings to the table directly clash with your natural will to live, stirring up a profound unease. Society often adds to this by treating it as a topic to be whispered about, if mentioned at all, making it feel even more like forbidden territory.

When existential dread creeps in, it's not uncommon to reach for defense mechanisms like denial to keep the angst at bay. And, if you look at it through the lens of evolution, prioritizing the here and now over pondering the great beyond has always made sense for survival. All these layers intertwine to nudge you away from dwelling on mortality. They help you to keep your psychological balance and savor the joys of life despite the shadow of its end lurking in the background.

But what if by contemplating your impermanence, you can strip away the trivial, the superficial, and the unnecessary, focusing instead on what truly matters? The idea of thinking about your end every single day might seem like a morbid concept at first. But you're not dwelling on death with dread but rather using this reflection as a tool to foster a deeper appreciation for life.

Seneca wrote:

Let us prepare our minds as if we'd come to the very end of life. Let us postpone nothing. Let us balance life's books each day... The one who puts the finishing touches on their life each day is never short of time. (Weaver, 2024)

This advice nudges you toward living every day as though it's your last—not by throwing caution to the wind but by fully valuing and making the most of each moment. It doesn't advise a grim obsession with dying. Rather, it's an invitation to fully embrace life in all its depth, vibrancy, and emotion. It can help you cultivate resilience, foster a deep sense of gratitude, and recognize the priceless value of the here and now.

The transient nature of the world around us is an invitation for continuous self-improvement and deeper connections with others. Everything is always changing, all of the time. So, use your thoughts to celebrate each day as a unique opportunity to grow and appreciate the beauty in fleeting moments, urging yourself to form a deeper connection to the present.

What Is Memento Mori?

The term *memento mori*, translated directly from Latin to "remember you will die," represents a long philosophical tradition that emphasizes the transient nature of human life and the importance of living with the awareness of our mortality. This concept, with roots dating back to ancient civilizations, is a powerful reminder to live virtuously and make the most of our fleeting existence.

The origins of the term can be traced back to Socrates, who regarded philosophy as a preparation for death. This tradition was carried forward by Stoic philosophers including Marcus Aurelius, who reflected on the immediacy of death to foster a life of virtue. His contemplations echo the sentiment that awareness of death should guide our actions, words, and thoughts in the present moment (Daily Stoic, 2017).

The visual representations of memento mori during the 17th century, particularly within the genre of Vanitas paintings, further illustrate this theme. Artists like Philippe de Champaigne used symbols such as skulls, hourglasses, and wilting flowers to convey life's fragility and the inevitability of death. These artworks served as reminders of mortality, encouraging viewers to reflect on their lives and the importance of living meaningfully.

In the modern era, the concept has been revitalized through various media, including literature, art, tattoos, and digital design, all of which serve as a bridge connecting the ancient world with contemporary society's reflections on life and death. The phrase not only underscores the universality of mortality but also highlights our role in crafting a life of significance and purpose, free from the trivialities that often consume our daily existence.

The relevance that remembering mortality holds today can be seen as a counterbalance to the often hedonistic and materialistic aspects of modern life. It is a sobering yet inspiring reminder that, despite our advancements and achievements, we are all bound by a common fate. This realization, rather than being morbid, can inspire a deeper appreciation for the present and a more profound commitment to living a life aligned with our values and aspirations.

Memento mori is a call to life—a reminder to live fully and with awareness and appreciation for the impermanence of our existence. It challenges us to consider what truly matters, to prioritize the essential over the ephemeral, and to embrace the full spectrum of human experience with courage and compassion.

The Stoics on Memento Mori

Stoicism teaches you to embrace the reality that everything is temporary, including your very existence. This isn't meant to dishearten you; rather, it's an encouragement to live more meaningfully and with purpose. Being aware that one day you will die is a powerful way to find peace. Thinking about the unfortunate things that could happen can help you appreciate what you have now. It helps you be thankful for the present and enjoy experiencing another day on Earth.

Prominent ancient Stoics also addressed the transience of life in their works. For example, Marcus Aurelius often contemplated the nature of life and death in his *Meditations*, urging us to live in harmony with the universe and to accept death as a natural part of life's cycle. Seneca, in his letters, discussed the shortness of life and the importance of living a life true to ourselves, one in which we are not swayed by external desires or concerns, including the fear of death. Epictetus emphasized the distinction between what is within our control and what isn't, teaching that peace comes from focusing on our actions and attitudes toward life and death rather than external circumstances.

By embracing the Stoic understanding of life's impermanence and the fleeting nature of external circumstances, you can view each new day as a precious opportunity to enhance your personal growth and deepen your relationships with others. Through this lens, challenges become opportunities to develop resilience, and every moment becomes a chance to act with kindness, integrity, and mindfulness and to enrich your life and the lives of those around you.

Marcus Aurelius

Marcus Aurelius contemplated the transient nature of life and the inevitability of death, urging us to live in alignment with nature and to accept death as an integral part of that nature. He advised us not to fear death but to see it as a natural process. He encouraged us to focus on living a life of virtue and to fulfill our duties, articulating this acceptance in his *Meditations* with:

Just that you do the right thing. The rest doesn't matter. Cold or warm. Tired or well-rested. Despised or honored. Dying ... or busy with other assignments. Because dying too is one of our assignments in life. There as well: "to do what needs doing." (Popova, 2015)

This quote encapsulates his Stoic belief in focusing on living virtuously, regardless of external circumstances. Aurelius's reflections are a reminder to embrace the present, act with integrity, and remember that, just as we are born with a purpose, so too is death a part of our life's work. Further of his notable insights include (*Marcus Aurelius Quotes*, n.d.):

- "Stop whatever you're doing for a moment and ask yourself: Am I afraid of death because I won't be able to do this anymore?"

- "Do not act as if you were going to live ten thousand years. Death hangs over you. While you live, while it is in your power, be good."

- "Perfection of character is this: to live each day as if it were your last, without frenzy, without apathy, without pretense."

Seneca

Seneca criticizes the allocation of significant time to superfluous activities, arguing that life's value does not depend on its duration but on our actions within it. Furthermore, his reflections on death emphasize that life's brevity is not inherent but a result of our misuse of time (The Stoic, 2021b). At the beginning of this book, we discussed that many of us live as though we have endless time, rarely acknowledging our mortality or the passage of time's effect on us. We often overlook how much time has already escaped us, treating it as infinite and, thus, we squander the moments that might be our last.

Seneca introduced the practice of *premeditatio malorum* to mentally prepare for adversity and enhance our satisfaction with what we have. It is a Stoic exercise and means "the premeditation of evils." It involves visualizing future hardships to prepare ourselves emotionally and practically for what we may lose—not unlike negative visualization. This practice strengthens resilience, diminishes the impact of negative events, and enhances gratitude for present circumstances.

The lessons this ancient Stoic imparted on preparation for poor outcomes and the impermanence of life encourage us to value our time, focus on meaningful activities, and cultivate a deep acceptance of life's fleeting nature. Adhering to Seneca's wisdom allows us to live more fully and with greater appreciation for the moments we have.

Some of his notable quotes on the subject are (*Seneca Quotes*, n.d.):

- "A man cannot live well if he knows not how to die well."

- "Let us postpone nothing. Let us balance life's books each day."

Epictetus

Epictetus also viewed death as a natural, inevitable part of life. He encouraged embracing death's reality, advising his followers not to fear it but to understand it as a component of life's nature. He believed this acknowledgment could liberate us from the fear of death, which would allow us to live more fully and with purpose. By contemplating death, he argued, we can focus on living according to virtue. We can make the most of the present by emphasizing the actions and thoughts that are within our control. This perspective can cultivate inner peace and resilience; it can guide us to live with dignity and calm amid life's uncertainties and inevitable end.

Epictetus's views on death are reflected in his own words (*Daily Stoic*, n.d.):

- "I must die, must I? If at once, then I am dying: if soon, I dine now, as it is time for dinner, and afterward when the time comes, I will die."

- "What is death? A scary mask. Take it off—see, it doesn't bite. Eventually, body and soul will have to separate, just as they existed separately before we were born. So, why be upset if it happens now? If it isn't now, it's later."

- "Death is not an evil. What is it then? The one law mankind has that is free of all discrimination."

Embracing Mortality: Insights From Contemporary Research

Recent studies and explorations have demonstrated the enduring relevance of these principles in our quest for a meaningful existence. At the heart of one strain of this discourse is memento mori, which Marcus Aurelius reflected upon in his *Meditations*. Bhandari's 2022 analysis of this and other Stoic virtues underscores their importance in navigating life's challenges with wisdom and ethical integrity, echoing Seneca's timeless advice to live each day as if it were our last.

In the realm of visual arts, Walter's investigation (2019) sheds light on how the depiction of memento mori transcends its perceived morbidity. Acknowledging the inevitability of death serves as a compelling invitation to reassess our time on Earth, and Walter suggests that these artistic expressions are not grim reminders but powerful catalysts for introspection. Echoing this sentiment, another study delves into the religious and secular interpretations of the term, highlighting its significance in fostering a deeper connection with the essence of our being across different cultural and spiritual landscapes (Riley, 2020).

The intersection of ancient wisdom and contemporary technology presents an intriguing avenue for reflection, as evidenced by work on incorporating memento mori into digital design. This innovative approach suggests that technology can offer new ways to engage with and reflect on our mortality, bridging the gap between age-old practices and modern-day experiences (Wallace et al., 2018).

How to Contemplate Your Own Death

As a method of shifting your mindset to the Stoic perspective, reflect on your mortality so that you may see each day as a gift. A practical method is to imagine crafting your obituary and working backward, like Warren Buffett suggests, to live a life aligned with your deepest values (Meier, n.d.). Also consider Jeff Bezos's leap into founding Amazon, motivated by his fear of regretting inaction more than failure. Ask yourself, as Steve Jobs did daily, if you'd be content doing your day's activities if it were your last. This direct engagement with memento mori can inspire you to live with intention and purpose.

To incorporate the concept into your life, implementing the following easy practices can help you live more purposefully and mindfully and make the most of each day with an acknowledgment of life's impermanence:

- **Perform daily reflections:** Spend a few minutes each morning contemplating the finite nature of life. This can instill a sense of urgency and purpose in your daily activities. You can incorporate this into your daily Stoic journaling practice with the following prompts:

  - Reflect on what activities or experiences you fear missing out on due to death. How will this influence your daily choices and priorities moving forward?

  - Consider Seneca's perspective: In fearing death, do you feel your current lifestyle truly differs from not living at all? What changes might you make to lead a more fulfilled life?

  - When you're embracing your loved ones, how does the

thought of their, or your, impermanence affect your appreciation and presence in those moments?

- **Do gratitude journaling:** Every day, write down three things you're grateful for. This practice can shift your focus to what truly matters, enhancing your appreciation for life's fleeting moments.

- **Set clear priorities:** Regularly review your goals and tasks, ensuring they align with your values and what you want to be remembered for.

- **Mindfulness moments:** Integrate brief mindfulness exercises into your day, such as deep breathing or mindful walking, to ground yourself in the present.

- **Carry a talisman:** Using a skull as a memento mori talisman is a traditional and powerful symbol to remind yourself of your mortality. It serves as a visual cue to reflect on the impermanence of life and the certainty of death, encouraging mindfulness and the prioritization of meaningful activities and relationships.

- **Recite a mantra:** As you settle in at night, whisper to yourself, "Today's journey is complete; I've lived fully within the bounds fate has drawn for me" (John, 2022a). This mantra serves as a gentle nudge to reflect on the day's experiences, acknowledging that each moment you have lived is a step completed on the path of life, a path shaped by both choice and destiny.

Reflecting on Impermanence

Contemplating death naturally leads us to embrace the broader concept of impermanence. This reflection deepens the understanding that not only our lives but all experiences, relationships, and material possessions are transient. By acknowledging our mortality, we can truly appreciate the fleeting nature of everything around us, fostering a deeper connection to the present moment and a more resilient, adaptable approach to life's inevitable changes. You do this when you:

- **Savor and appreciate present moments:** Recognize the transient beauty and joy of life, which is like the fleeting beauty of a vase filled with fresh-cut peonies. Blooming magnificently for only a few days, these flowers serve as a vivid example of the passing joys and beauty surrounding us.

- **Reframe positively:** Adopt a positive mindset toward change, seeing it as an opportunity for growth and new experiences. Acknowledging that impermanence exists and is out of your control can bring you peace and help you be mindful of the current moment.

- **Reflect on different resolutions:** Consider impermanence from various perspectives, from the macroscopic view of life and death to the microscopic changes in each moment, to cultivate a deeper understanding and acceptance of constant change (Bodhipaksa, 2012).

Being More Present

Acknowledging the temporary nature of external circumstances underlines the significance of being present. This awareness fosters a deeper appreciation for the transient beauty of life, urging us to seize each day as an opportunity for self-improvement and enriching our relationships. It encourages us to open ourselves to the full spectrum of experiences life offers, turning everyday moments into chances for growth and deeper connections, thus living more fully and meaningfully as our ideal selves.

You can practice being more present by:

- **Focusing on breathing:** Engage in exercises that center your attention on your breath, as this aids in anchoring you to the present moment.

- **Doing meditation practices:** Regular meditation helps calm your mind, enhancing your awareness of your current experience.

- **Limiting social media use:** Reducing time spent on social platforms can decrease distractions, allowing for increased engagement with your immediate environment.

- **Staying connected with your body:** Physical activities or mindfulness exercises can strengthen your connection to bodily sensations, promoting your sense of presence.

- **Accepting uncertainty:** Embracing the fact that not all questions have answers can reduce your anxiety over the future, helping you to focus more on the now.

Interactive Element

15-Second Memento Mori Meditation

This tool serves as a reminder to reflect on the time you've spent living and the time you have remaining, all within a quick 15-second check-in each week. It's a physical diagram that visualizes the progression of your life over time.

To complete the exercise, you'll have to create a chart. For this, you'll need to draw a grid with 80 rows and 52 columns. Each row represents one year, and each column represents one week. This layout covers the typical span of a human life. Begin by writing your birth date in the top left corner and filling in the squares up to the current week. At the end of each week, mark off one square for one week of your life. You can use an "x," or color it in. Continue to fill in one cell for every week that passes, keeping the visualization of your life's progression current. You will see the page fill up slowly as the weeks go by.

As you fill in each square, reflect on how you have used your time. Ask yourself if you were satisfied with how you spent it. If the answer is yes, that's wonderful. If not, the chart serves its purpose by pushing you to consider why and how you might live more meaningfully. It's a tool for self-reflection, encouraging you to think about whether your actions align with your values and goals.

Applying Stoic Wisdom

Imagine, for a moment, what life would be like without your parent. This exercise is not meant to be morbid but rather to enhance your awareness and acceptance of life's impermanence. It urges us to make the most of the time we have with loved ones. Doing this reflection can therefore motivate you to engage more fully in your relationship, to express love and gratitude for your parent openly, and to not leave important words unsaid.

Many of us either know or will learn that caring for a sick parent is undoubtedly challenging. However, it also offers a unique opportunity for growth and reflection, especially when it's viewed through the lens of memento mori. This perspective can help us focus on what's truly important, encouraging us to cherish the present moments with our loved ones.

Simple yet meaningful actions can make a significant difference in this journey. Spending quality, undistracted time with your parent, listening to their stories, and creating new memories together can strengthen your bond and provide comfort during tough times. Practicing gratitude daily by noting down simple joys, such as a shared smile or a quiet moment together, can shift your focus to the positive aspects of life, even amid hardship. Documenting this journey, whether through journaling or photos, can be therapeutic and create a lasting memento of the time spent together.

When you are a caretaker, self-care is crucial; it enables you to support your parent more effectively. Engaging in activities that replenish your spirit, whether it's a hobby or exercise, is essential for maintaining your well-being. Additionally, seeking support from others in similar situations through support groups or online communities can provide comfort and valuable advice. Flexibility and adaptability are also key in navigating the unpredictability of caregiving. Plans may change and learning to go with the flow can reduce stress.

Open communication with your parent about fears, wishes, and hopes ensures their desires are honored, and it fosters a deeper connection. Daily mindfulness practices, like focusing on your breath, can help manage stress and bring your attention back to the present, where peace often resides. Despite the circumstances, it's important to seek out moments of joy and laughter, which can lighten the mood and offer respite.

Building upon what we discussed in Chapter 5, incorporating the practice of negative visualization can further enrich your caregiving journey. By contemplating the possibility of your parent's passing, not with a sense of dread but as a form of mental preparation, you can deepen your appreciation for the present moments shared with them. This practice, while seemingly counterintuitive, encourages a form of emotional resilience, preparing you for future hardships and helping you cherish the time you have now even more.

Conclusion

Essentially, memento mori prompts us to ask ourselves daily: If today were my last, am I living in a way that would leave a legacy of love, wisdom, and a life well-lived?

The acceptance of death as part of the human experience can bring a sense of peace and clarity. It helps strip away the trivial concerns that often occupy our minds, focusing our attention on what truly matters. In embracing the full spectrum of the human experience, including the inevitability of loss, we learn to live more fully and meaningfully.

This concept isn't meant to darken our days with thoughts of dying but to highlight the beauty, opportunities, and potential in each moment. It encourages us to strive for self-improvement, not only in pursuing our goals fervently but also in appreciating and nurturing the relationships and experiences that give depth and meaning to life. The Stoic practice of contemplating our impermanence therefore guides us toward a life of authenticity, resilience, and mindful presence.

Conclusion

T he aspects of Stoicism presented in this book have given you practical ways to grow stronger, happier, and closer to your ideal self, no matter what life throws at you. The lessons imparted have taught you that if you focus on what you can control—your thoughts, feelings, and actions—you can find peace and fulfillment, even during the toughest times. At the heart of Stoicism, as you have learned, is the idea that how we react to things matters more than the things themselves.

You should now know that contrary to popular belief, Stoicism isn't about not caring; it's about living fully, experiencing all there is to life with a clear mind and strong morals. The Stoics remind us that living according to virtues like wisdom, courage, justice, and moderation fosters habits for a life that you can work on daily. By practicing these values, you can face your fears, overcome challenges, and live a more peaceful and meaningful life.

Stoicism can transform your approach to life's challenges and the way you respond to them. It shows you that your happiness and fulfillment come from how you react and see things, not from what happens around you. Instead of seeing difficulties as barriers, you can learn to see them as opportunities for growth and learning. This shift in perspective is freeing. It motivates you to welcome tough times as teachers that guide you to become more resilient, emotionally balanced, and deeply connected to the present. By embracing this way of thinking, you build a life filled with peace, meaning, and alignment with your core values.

The guidance in this book has gone beyond just presenting new knowledge. It has introduced small, impactful changes in your life that can shift your mindset. Let these suggestions inspire you to tweak your daily habits and behaviors. Incorporating basic Stoic principles into your everyday life can bring you closer to the person you aspire to be. This development is not only about altering your thought patterns but also about aligning your actions with your values.

When your behavior reflects your beliefs, you pave the way for genuine self-improvement. Consistently evaluating your principles and living by them, I trust, will lead you to become your best self. This straightforward, actionable approach demystifies the process of self-improvement. Keep your mindset to personal growth simple, as the path to a more fulfilling life consists of the daily choices you make. Be purposeful with how you spend your time and choose activities that truly make your life better.

It takes some time to learn to see life's challenges not as obstacles but as chances to grow stronger, build better relationships, and become more resilient. The Stoic approach helps you focus on your actions and reactions, building a strength inside you that stays constant, no matter where you are or what you are going through. Worrying about things that are outside your control is just a waste of your energy. It might be tough, but adopting a Stoic mindset can guide you to get better at it until it becomes a natural part of who you are.

Implementing Stoic journaling by following the guidance in this book can significantly impact your daily life. Beyond mere reflection, it serves as a tool for aligning your actions with your core values and shifting focus from external validation to personal growth. Journaling encourages introspection, allowing you to form a clearer understanding of your desires and principles, and it fosters a deliberate approach to making life choices.

The practice offers multiple benefits, including enhanced emotional intelligence and stress relief. It provides a space to articulate thoughts and feelings, leading to better emotional management and a calmer approach to challenges. Additionally, it cultivates gratitude, shifting your perspective toward abundance and appreciation.

To make Stoic journaling a part of your routine, choose a medium that suits your lifestyle, be it a notebook or a digital device. Consistency is key to harnessing the full benefits of this practice. Over time, this habit not only deepens your engagement with Stoic principles but also promotes a more authentic, value-driven life.

In closing, it's crucial to underline the VIRTUE framework's role as your compass through Stoic philosophy's vast landscape. The components—*veto* the uncontrollable, *inspire* your ideal self, *roll* with the punches, *turn* obstacles into opportunities, *unburden* yourself from the unnecessary, and *embrace* the ephemeral nature of existence—serve not merely as philosophical concepts but as actionable steps toward a more balanced and fulfilling life. Each element of the framework invites you to actively engage with the world, your challenges, and your aspirations in a manner that aligns with Stoic wisdom.

By internalizing and applying these principles, you embark on a transformative journey toward resilience, peace, and purpose. This framework empowers you to navigate life's unpredictability with grace, harnessing every experience as a catalyst for personal growth and deeper understanding. As you move forward, let VIRTUE be your guide, reminding you that the essence of a rich and meaningful life lies in your responses to the world around you. In adopting this Stoic mindset, you lay the foundation for a life marked by continuous learning, emotional strength, and unwavering commitment to your highest ideals.

Reaching the end of this book marks a new beginning for you. If Stoicism was a fresh concept to you, you now have the opportunity to weave ancient wisdom into your daily life. If you already had some understanding of it, you've now deepened your knowledge and discovered new ways to apply it.

If this journey has brought you any enlightenment, I encourage you to share your experiences with others by leaving a review of this book. Your insights might just be the beacon that leads someone else to the transformative change they're seeking. Remember, your journey is only just starting. It's a small act with a big impact, and together, we can enrich the journey for others.

To leave your review, simply scan the QR code below. Thank you for sharing your journey with us and for helping to spread the timeless lessons of Stoicism.

Glossary

Amor fati: The love of our fate; embracing everything that happens, including suffering and loss, with a positive and accepting attitude.

Decluttering: Although not explicitly defined, the term implies removing unnecessary items from our lives to focus on what truly matters, in line with Stoic simplicity and moderation.

Dichotomy of control: Distinguishing between what is and isn't within our control, focusing our energy on what we can change, and accepting what we cannot.

Ethics: The branch of philosophy that deals with what is morally right and wrong, guiding how we make decisions and live our lives.

Eudaemonia: Central to Stoic philosophy, this term refers to a state of flourishing or happiness achieved by living in accordance with reason and human nature.

Existentialism: A term that generally refers to a philosophy that emphasizes individual freedom, choice, and existential angst.

Four virtues: Wisdom, justice, courage, and temperance are classified as the main types of virtue in Stoicism, and they guide ethical living.

Gratitude: The practice of being thankful and appreciating what we have to foster contentment and positive relationships with ourselves and others.

Growth mindset: While not explicitly defined, this implies an attitude that embraces learning and development, consistent with Stoic principles of self-improvement.

Impermanence: The concept that all things are temporary, encouraging appreciation of the present and acceptance of change.

Locus of control: The degree to which we believe we have control over the outcome of events in our lives, with Stoicism advocating an internal locus of control.

Marcus Aurelius: A Roman Emperor and Stoic philosopher who wrote *Meditations*. He emphasized virtue, duty, and rationality in governance and personal conduct.

Memento mori: The reflection on mortality and reminding ourselves that death is inevitable, which encourages living a meaningful and virtuous life.

Moderation: Exercising self-control and restraint in all aspects of life. to maintain balance and align with Stoic virtue.

Negative visualization: The practice of contemplating potential negative outcomes to appreciate what we have and prepare for adversity.

Philosophy: The study of fundamental questions about existence, knowledge, values, reason, mind, and language, with Stoicism being a branch focusing on virtue and wisdom.

Resilience: The ability to endure and adapt to adversity, maintaining inner tranquility and purposeful action despite external events.

Seneca: A Stoic philosopher who advocated living a life aligned with nature and reason and who emphasized moral integrity and the value of simplicity.

Stoicism: A philosophical belief system that emphasizes living in harmony with nature, advocating self-control and resilience to overcome harmful emotions.

References

Ackerman, C. E. (2018, October 22). *How to live in the present moment: 35 exercises and tools (+ Quotes)*. PositivePsychology.com. https://positi vepsychology.com/present-moment/

Alaili, A. (2022, April 21). *You act like mortals in all that you fear, and like immortals in all that you desire—Seneca*. Entrepreneur Post. https://www.entrepreneurpost.com/2022/04/21/you-act-like-mort als-in-all-that-you-fear-and-like-immortals-in-all-that-you-desire -seneca/

Andersen, C. H. (2023, January 9). *7 simple ways to practice gratitude in your everyday life*. Reader's Digest. https://www.rd.com/article/how -to-practice-gratitude/

Astoul, E. (2023, September 28). *How to want less and be happy about it? 9 brilliant tips to apply*. Green With Less. https://greenwithless.com /how-want-less-be-happy/

Atlas, M. I. (2021, April 27). *5 myths about Stoicism that you should be aware of*. LinkedIn. https://www.linkedin.com/pulse/5-myths-stoic ism-you-should-aware-max-ignatius-atlas

Attard, A. (2021, May 6). *Accepting impermanence can help us live more flexibly*. Psychology Today. https://www.psychologytoday.com/us/blog/human-beings-being -human/202105/accepting-impermanence-can-help-us-live-more-f lexibly

Barbosa, C. (2020, September 24). *Misconceptions about Stoicism*. The Wise Mind. https://thewisemind.net/misconceptions-about-stoic ism/

Bennett, S. (2021, September 6). *3 methods to want less in life (and be happy with less)*. Tracking Happiness. https://www.trackinghappin ess.com/how-to-want-less/

Bhandari, S. R. (2022). Amor fati and memento mori in Marcus Aure-lius' *Meditations*: The synthesis of Stoicism. *Journal of NELTA Gan-daki, 5*(1–2), 17–29. https://doi.org/10.3126/jong.v5i1-2.49277

Bodhipaksa. (2012, December 23). *Six ways of reflecting on imperma-nence*. Wildmind. https://www.wildmind.org/blogs/on-practice/ref lecting-on-impermanence

Brodsky, G. M. (1998). Nietzsche's notion of amor fati. *Continental Philosophy Review, 31*(1), 35–57. https://doi.org/10.1023/a:10100775 19649

Brooks, J. (2019, September 7). *The dichotomy of control*. The Stoic Hand-book. https://www.stoichandbook.co/the-dichotomy-of-control/

Brooks, J. (2020, September 10). *Meditation: The dichotomy of control training*. The Stoic Handbook. https://stoicism.substack.com/p/me ditation-the-dichotomy-of-control#details

Buckley, D. (2018, November 12). *How to deal with failure and pick your-self back up*. Lifehack. https://www.lifehack.org/814095/how-to-de al-with-failure

Bush, R. A. (2021, January 9). *Stoicism and desire regulation*. Mod-ern Stoicism. https://modernstoicism.com/stoicism-and-desire-re gulation-by-ryan-bush/

Camp, S. (2020, December 28). *Develop your locus of control: 4 Tactics to become the master of your reality*. Unstoppable Rise. https://www.un stoppablerise.com/internal-locus-of-control/

Carol Dweck: A summary of the two mindsets. (2015, March 2). Farnam Street. https://fs.blog/carol-dweck-mindset/

Chen, G. (2020, May 10). *A Stoic guide on the dichotomy of control and happiness.* The Stoic Sage. https://thestoicsage.com/dichoto my-of-control/

Chew, L. (2018, March 1). *9 Stoic practices that will help you thrive in the madness of modernity.* Daily Stoic. https://dailystoic.com/stoi cism-modernity/

Cloward, E. (2021, September 6). *Life is long if you know how to use it.* Stoic Coffee Break. https://stoic.coffee/blog/202-life-is-long -if-you-know-how-to-use-it/

Colins, A. (2023, May 30). *Slow decluttering: The benefits of decluttering slowly.* Balance Through Simplicity. https://balancethroughs implicity.com/slow-decluttering/

Crawford, C. A., & Helm, B. M. (2019). How can Stoic philosophy inspire psychosocial genetic counseling practice? An introduction and exploration. *Journal of Rational-Emotive & Cognitive-Behavior Therapy.* https://doi.org/10.1007/s10942-019-00330-6

Cullum, D. (2021, August 15). *Seneca Sundays: On facing hardships—Letter 96.* Dan's Daily. https://dancullum.com/2021/08/s eneca-sundays-on-facing-hardships-letter-96/

Cuncic, A. (2021, November 10). *How do you live in the present?* Verywell Mind. https://www.verywellmind.com/how-do-you-live-i n-the-present-5204439

Daily Stoic. (n.d.). *Epictetus Quotes.* https://dailystoic.com/epictetu s-quotes/

Daily Stoic. (2017a, January 23). *Who is Zeno? An introduction to the founder of Stoicism.* https://dailystoic.com/zeno/

Daily Stoic. (2017b, October 25). *A Stoic response to mean or selfish people.* https://dailystoic.com/stoic-response-mean-selfish-peo ple/

Daily Stoic. (2017c, December 12). *What is memento mori?* https://d ailystoic.com/what-is-memento-mori/

Daily Stoic. (2018, September 8). *Who is Gaius Musonius Rufus? Getting to know "The Roman Socrates."* https://dailystoic.com/musonius-rufus/

Daily Stoic. (2019a, March 27). *Who is Marcus Aurelius? Getting to know the Roman Emperor.* https://dailystoic.com/marcus-aurelius/

Daily Stoic. (2019b, December 30). *7 Stoic practices to help you become your ideal self in 2020.* https://dailystoic.com/7-stoic-practices-to-ideal-self/

Daily Stoic. (2020a, February 7). *5 Stoic lessons on time management.* https://dailystoic.com/time-management/

Daily Stoic. (2020b, March 24). *Time management: 6 techniques from the Stoic philosopher Seneca.* https://dailystoic.com/time-management-6-techniques-from-the-stoic-philosopher-seneca/

Daily Stoic. (2021, July 13). *5 Stoic tips for handling rude people.* https://dailystoic.com/5-stoic-tips-for-handling-rude-people/

Daskal, L. (2016, June 22). *19 highly effective ways to stay motivated.* Inc.com. https://www.inc.com/lolly-daskal/19-simple-ways-to-stay-motivated-that-actually-work.html

Davenport, B. (2022, November 28). *11 practices to help you let go of ego.* Mindful Zen. https://mindfulzen.co/let-go-of-ego/

Davies, S. (2020, May 5). *Slow decluttering.* A Considered Life. https://www.aconsideredlife.co.uk/2020/05/slow-decluttering.html

Dong, X., Li, X., Jiang, X., & Xiang, Y. (2022). How does mindfulness relate to benign/malicious envy? The mediating role of resilience, internal locus of control and self-esteem. *Frontiers in Psychiatry, 13.* https://doi.org/10.3389/fpsyt.2022.878690

Donghia, M. (2023, August 10). *How to systematically declutter your life.* Becoming Minimalist. https://www.becomingminimalist.com/how-to-systematically-declutter-your-life/

Eason, A. (2018, April 17). *How to embrace impermanence and why it is so important.* Adam Eason. https://www.adam-eason.com/embrace-impermanence-important/

Elgat, G. (2016). Amor fati as practice: How to love fate. *The Southern Journal of Philosophy, 54*(2), 174–188. https://doi.org/10.1111/sjp.12171

Favreau, M. (n.d.). *Finding balance: How to practice moderation.* Wise Bread. https://www.wisebread.com/finding-balance-how-to-practice-moderation

Ferguson, S. (2022, September 12). *Living in the moment: 7 tips for being more present.* Psych Central. https://psychcentral.com/blog/what-it-really-means-to-be-in-the-present-moment

Five ways to practise gratitude every day. (2023, December 5). AIA. https://www.aia.com/en/health-wellness/healthy-living/healthy-mind/Practise-gratitude

Fletcher, D., & Sarkar, M. (2013). Psychological resilience: A review and critique of definitions, concepts and theory. *European Psychologist, 18*(1), 12–23. https://doi.org/10.1027/1016-9040/a000124

Fran. (2022, April 25). *What is a growth mindset and how can you develop one?* FutureLearn. https://www.futurelearn.com/info/blog/general/develop-growth-mindset

Ghezelbash, P. (2017, September 5). *The philosophy of Stoicism: 4 lessons from antiquity on self-discipline.* Daily Stoic. https://dailystoic.com/self-discipline/

Handley, D. (2015, August 10). *Life is long, if you know how to use it.* LinkedIn. https://www.linkedin.com/pulse/life-long-you-know-how-use-derek-handley

Hanselman, S. (2020, October 3). *The 9 core Stoic beliefs.* Daily Stoic. https://dailystoic.com/9-core-stoic-beliefs/

Harte, E. (2021, August 7). *Memento mori: From the guise of the ancients to 21st century practice.* Modern Sto-

icism. https://modernstoicism.com/memento-mori-from-the-guis
e-of-the-ancients-to-21st-century-practice-by-enda-harte/

HealthDirect. (2018, March 9). *Motivation: How to get started and staying motivated.* HealthDirect Australia. https://www.healthdirect.gov.au
/motivation-how-to-get-started-and-staying-motivated

Herselman, K. (2023, February 27). *Modern Stoicism as an answer to life and business challenges.* LinkedIn. https://www.linkedin.com/pulse/modern-stoicism-ans
wer-life-business-challenges-koos-herselman

Ho, L. (2020, January 21). *17 ways to develop a growth mindset.* Lifehack. https://www.lifehack.org/861739/17-ways-to-develop-a-gro
wth-mindset

Holiday, R. (2009, April 1). *The obstacle becomes the way.* Ryan Holiday. https://ryanholiday.net/the-obstacle-becomes-the-way/

How Stoicism can help you achieve personal growth. (n.d.). Stoic Simple. https://www.stoicsimple.com/how-stoicism-can-help-you-ac
hieve-personal-growth/

How to make personal reflection a powerful daily habit. (2019, December 26). Day Designer. https://daydesigner.com/a/blog/how-to-make
-personal-reflection-a-powerful-daily-habit

Hufford, B. (2017, January 27). *Amor fati: The immense power of learning to love your fate.* Daily Stoic. https://dailystoic.com/amor-fati/

Hughes, A. J. (2017, December 6). *8 Stoic secrets to help you build mental toughness.* Daily Stoic. https://dailystoic.com/stoic-secrets-for-men
tal-toughness/

Intelligent Change. (2023). *What is growth mindset and how to achieve it.* Intelligent Change. https://www.intelligentchange.com/blogs/r
ead/what-is-growth-mindset-and-how-to-achieve-it

Inzlicht, M., Legault, L., & Teper, R. (2014). Exploring the mechanisms of self-control improvement. *Current Directions in Psychological Science, 23*(4), 302–307. https://doi.org/10.1177/0963721414534256

Isaacs, D. (2023). Control and Stoicism. *Journal of Paediatrics and Child Health, 59*(5), 709–710. https://doi.org/10.1111/jpc.16300

Jesper. (2020, August 16). *The Stoic dichotomy of control to calm your mind.* Mind & Practice. https://mindandpractice.com/calm-your-mind-with-the-stoic-dichotomy-of-control/

John, A. (2018, February 9). *How to practice Stoic negative visualisation.* What Is Stoicism? https://whatisstoicism.com/stoicism-definition/how-to-practice-stoic-negative-visualisation/

John, A. (2022a, January 9). *What is memento mori?* What Is Stoicism? https://whatisstoicism.com/stoicism-definition/what-is-memento-mori/

John, A. (2022b, March 13). *What is the dichotomy of control?* What Is Stoicism? https://whatisstoicism.com/stoicism-definition/what-is-the-dichotomy-of-control/

John, A. (2022c, September 11). *Understanding this misconception could change how you think about Stoicism.* What Is Stoicism? https://whatisstoicism.com/stoicism-resources/understanding-this-misconception-could-change-how-you-think-about-stoicism/

Kapageridis, Y. (2020, May 11). *Resilience lessons from Stoicism.* SAFETY4SEA. https://safety4sea.com/resilience-lessons-from-stoicism/

Kathy. (2020, May 13). *5 Stoic questions to ask yourself daily.* Minimalist Focus. https://minimalistfocus.com/5-stoic-questions-to-ask-yourself-daily/

Kristenson, S. (2022, August 18). *Amor fati: How to apply this philosophy to your life.* Happier Human. https://www.happierhuman.com/amor-fati/

Lake, T. (2022, December 20). *An in-depth understanding on the four virtues of Stoicism.* The Collector. https://www.thecollector.com/four-cardinal-virtues-stoicism/

Lalonde, J. (2023, June 16). *25 questions to ask yourself when you fail.* Joseph Lalonde. https://www.jmlalonde.com/25-questions -to-ask-yourself-when-you-fail/

Lambert, S. M., Moore, D. W., & Dixon, R. S. (1999). Gymnasts in training: The differential effects of self-and coach-set goals as a function of locus of control. *Journal of Applied Sport Psychology,* *11*(1), 72–82. https://doi.org/10.1080/10413209908402951

Lesso, R. (2022, July 1). *What are the origins of Stoicism?* The Collector. https://www.thecollector.com/what-are-the-origins-of-sto icism-history/

Lonczak, H. (2020, November 17). *36 ways to find a silver lining during challenging times.* PositivePsychology.com. https://positivepsych ology.com/find-a-silver-lining/

MacRae, B. (2021, March 28). *Be more resilient: 9 Stoic practices.* The Mindful Stoic. https://mindfulstoic.net/how-to-be-resilient-res etting-promptly/

MacRae, B. (2023, June 25). *How to practice amor fati: Turning fate into your ally.* The Mindful Stoic. https://mindfulstoic.net/how-t o-practice-amor-fati/

Maden, J. (2021, June). *Seneca on coping with the shortness of life.* Philosophy Break. https://philosophybreak.com/articles/seneca -on-coping-with-the-shortness-of-life/

Maden, J. (2023, December). *Amor fati: the Stoics' and Nietzsche's different takes on loving fate.* Philosophy Break. https://philosophybreak.com/articles/amor-fati-the-stoi cs-and-nietzsche-different-takes-on-loving-fate/

Mark, J. J. (2014, August 11). *The life and thought of Zeno of Citium in Diogenes Laertius.* World History Encyclopedia. https://www.worldhistory.org/article/741/the-life-and-tho ught-of-zeno-of-citium-in-diogenes/

Marcus Aurelius quotes. (n.d.) Goodreads. https://www.goodreads.com /author/quotes/17212.Marcus_Aurelius

Masten, A. S., Best, K. M., & Garmezy, N. (1990). Resilience and development: Contributions from the study of children who overcome adversity. *Development and Psychopathology, 2*(4), 425. https://doi.or g/10.1017/s0954579400005812

Mather Hospital. (2017, April 19). *Spring cleaning: 5 health benefits to decluttering your life.* =https://www.matherhospital.org/wellness-at-mather/health-well ness/spring-cleaning-5-health-benefits-to-decluttering-your-life/

Meier, J. D. (n.d.). *Memento mori: Shaping your life with purpose.* Sources of Insight. https://sourcesofinsight.com/memento-mori/

Memento mori: Why remembering death will change your life. (n.d.). Stoic Store UK. https://stoicstore.co.uk/memento-mori/

Miles, J. (2022, September 1). *How to manage time: The wisdom of the Stoics.* Passion Struck. https://johnrmiles.com/how-to-manage-time-the-wisdom-of-the -stoics/#:~:text=Roman%20stoic%20philosopher%20Lucius%20Se neca

Mitchell, C. E. (1989). Internal locus of control for expectation, perception, and management of answered prayer. *Journal of Psychology and Theology, 17*(1), 21–26. https://doi.org/10.1177/009164718901700105

Mollison, J. A. (2018). Nietzsche contra Stoicism: Naturalism and value, suffering, and amor fati. *Inquiry, 62*(1), 93–115. https://doi.org/10.10 80/0020174x.2019.1527547

Morin, A. (2022, May 23). *The best way to boost your motivation when you just aren't feeling it.* Verywell Mind. https://www.verywellmind.com /what-to-do-when-you-have-no-motivation-4796954

Mount, J. (2021, May 11). *How to gain mental clarity & productivity from Stoicism.* Mind & Practice. https://mindandpractice.com/how-to-g ain-mental-clarity-productivity-from-stoicism/

Nair, S. (2023a, June 12). *Stoic journaling—how to apply the philosophy of Stoicism into your journaling.* Journey Blog. https://blog.journey.cloud/stoic-journaling-how-to-apply-the-philosophy-of-stoicism-into-your-journaling/

Nair, S. (2023b, September 20). *50 Stoic journaling prompts examples.* Journey Blog. https://blog.journey.cloud/50-stoic-journaling-prompts-example/

Newsonen, S. (2022, September 23). *4 ways to see the silver lining in anything.* Psychology Today. https://www.psychologytoday.com/intl/blog/the-path-passionate-happiness/202208/4-ways-see-the-silver-lining-in-anything

Ng, T. W. H., Sorensen, K. L., & Eby, L. T. (2006). Locus of control at work: A meta-analysis. *Journal of Organizational Behavior, 27*(8), 1057–1087. https://doi.org/10.1002/job.416

Oppong, T. (2023, March 15). *Stoic journaling: A tool for reflection & discovery.* Hive. https://hive.com/blog/stoic-journaling/#:~:text=Regularly%20journaling%20allows%20Stoics%20to

Paquette, R. (2019, February 7). *20 Stoic journal topics for self-development.* Reggie Paquette. https://regpaq.com/stoic-journal-topics

Parkhurst, E., & Beckwith, A. (2022, July 1). *The mental health benefits of decluttering.* Utah State University. https://extension.usu.edu/mentalhealth/articles/the-mental-benefits-of-decluttering

Popova, M. (2015, November 18). *Marcus Aurelius on mortality and the key to living fully.* The Marginalian. https://www.themarginalian.org/2015/11/18/marcus-aurelius-meditations-mortality/

Prasetyo, F. (2022, April 16). *100 journal prompts for self acceptance and validation.* Lifengoal. https://lifengoal.com/journal-prompts-for-self-acceptance/

Riley, A. (2020). Kobe Bryant, memento mori: Death, religion, philosophy, basketball. *Society, 57*(6), 627–630. https://doi.org/10.1007/s12115-020-00542-y

Robertson, D. J. (2022, August 2). *How Stoicism could help you build resilience.* Psychology Today. https://www.psychologytoday.com/us/blog/the-psychology-stoicism/202208/how-stoicism-could-help-you-build-resilience

Rose, R. (2023, February 25). *Questions to ask yourself after failure.* Your Perfect Dreams. https://www.yourperfectdreams.com/questions-to-ask-yourself-after-failure/

Roy, S. (2021, September 6). *Amor fati: Stoic practice to soar above the volatile times.* The Happiness Blog. https://happyproject.in/amor-fati/

Sadler, G. (2018, February 10). *Stoicism, erotic love, and relationships.* Modern Stoicism. https://modernstoicism.com/stoicism-erotic-love-and-relationships-by-greg-sadler/

Salzgeber, J. (2019, May 16). *The easiest way to explain Stoicism: The Stoic happiness triangle.* NJlifehacks. https://www.njlifehacks.com/explain-stoicism-the-stoic-happiness-triangle/

Samuels, S. (2017, September 9). *How to practice moderation.* Simone Samuels. https://www.simonesamuels.com/blog/how-to-practice-moderation/2017/9/8

Schaffner, A. K. (2023, June 1). *Understanding the circles of influence, concern, and control.* PositivePsychology.com. https://positivepsychology.com/circles-of-influence/

Seneca. (n.d.). *On conquering the conqueror* (R.M. Gummere, Trans.). Monadnock Valley Press. https://monadnock.net/seneca/30.html

Seneca. (n.d.). *On the vanity of mental gymnastics* (R.M. Gummere, Trans.). Monadnock Valley Press. https://monadnock.net/seneca/111.html

Seneca. (n.d.) *On the vanity of place-seeking* (R.M. Gummere, Trans.). Monadnock Valley Press. https://monadnock.net/seneca/118.html

Seneca. (n.d.). *On true and false riches* (R.M. Gummere, Trans.). Monadnock Valley Press. https://monadnock.net/seneca/110.html

Seneca quotes. (n.d.). Goodreads. https://www.goodreads.com/aut
hor/quotes/4918776.Seneca

Shevchuk, D. (2023). Stoicism as philosophy of existential resilience. *Scientific Notes of the National University Ostroh Academy
Series Philosophy, 1*(24), 55–60. https://doi.org/10.25264/2312-71
12-2023-24-55-60

Sloane, P. (2014). *5 great questions to ask yourself after a failure.*
https://willamette.edu/arts-sciences/dean/student-resources/st
udent-success/pdf/5-great-questions-to-ask-yourself-after-a-fa
ilure.pdf

Smith, J. (2020, September 25). *Growth mindset vs fixed mindset: How
what you think affects what you achieve.* Mindset Health. https://w
ww.mindsethealth.com/matter/growth-vs-fixed-mindset

The Stoic. (2020a, February 11). *Letter I. On saving time.* The Stoic
Letters. https://thestoicletters.com/letter-i-on-saving-time/

The Stoic. (2020b, February 11). *Letter III. On true and false friendship.*
The Stoic Letters. https://thestoicletters.com/letter-iii-on-true
-and-false-friendship/

The Stoic. (2020c, February 12). *Letter V. On the philosopher's mean.*
The Stoic Letters. https://thestoicletters.com/letter-v-on-the-p
hilosophers-mean/

The Stoic. (2020d, April 13). *Letter XVII. On philosophy and riches.*
The Stoic Letters. https://thestoicletters.com/seneca-letter-xvii
-wealth-stoicism-on-philosophy-and-riches/

The Stoic. (2020e, May 12). *Letter XX. On practising what you preach.*
The Stoic Letters. https://thestoicletters.com/letter-xx-on-prac
tising-what-you-preach/

The Stoic. (2020f, October 5). *Letter XXXIX. On noble aspirations.* The
Stoic Letters. https://thestoicletters.com/seneca-letter-xxxix-o
n-noble-aspirations/

The Stoic. (2021a, January 22). *Letter XLIII. On the relativity of fame*. The Stoic Letters. https://thestoicletters.com/letter-xliii-on-the-relativity-of-fame/

The Stoic. (2021b, March 12). *Letter XLIX. On the shortness of life*. The Stoic Letters. https://thestoicletters.com/letter-xlix-on-the-shortness-of-life/

Stoic quotes on fame and vanity. (n.d.). iPerceptive. https://iperceptive.com/quotes/stoicism-fame-vanity.html

Stoic ways to build resilience in tough times. (n.d.). Stoic. https://www.getstoic.com/blog/stoic-ways-to-build-resilience-in-tough-times

Stoics believe that everything that happens is perfect. (2020, November 25). Exploring Your Mind. https://exploringyourmind.com/stoics-believe-that-everything-that-happens-is-perfect/

Straw, E. (2023, November 10). *Become the best version of yourself*. Success Starts Within. https://www.successstartswithin.com/blog/becoming-the-best-version-of-yourself-crafting-your-ideal-self-image

Tan, S.-Y. (2013). Resilience and posttraumatic growth: Empirical evidence and clinical applications from a Christian perspective. *Journal of Psychology and Christianity, 32*(4). https://psycnet.apa.org/record/2014-02248-010

The impact of daily routines on personal growth and job satisfaction. (2023, June 20). Loving Life. https://lovinglifeco.com/personal-growth/the-impact-of-daily-routines-on-personal-growth-and-job-satisfaction/

Thomas, L. J., & Asselin, M. (2018). Promoting resilience among nursing students in clinical education. *Nurse Education in Practice, 28*(28), 231–234. https://doi.org/10.1016/j.nepr.2017.10.001

Thomson, J. (2021, October 15). *The power to choose: How Stoicism approaches toxic relationships*. Big Think. https://bigthink.com/thinking/stoicism-toxic-relationships/

Tsatiris, D. (2022, May 15). *How to be happy with less.* Psychology Today. https://www.psychologytoday.com/us/blog/anxiety-in-high-achievers/202205/how-be-happy-less

Ursulean, M. (2022, March 17). *A guide to the 4 Stoic virtues: The modern individual's moral compass.* The Stoic Optimizer. https://thestoicoptimizer.com/4-stoic-virtues/

Van Treuren, P. (n.d.). *What the heck foes "eudaimonia" mean?* Stoic Simple. https://www.stoicsimple.com/what-the-heck-does-eudaimonia-mean/

Wallace, J., Thomas, J., Anderson, D., & Olivier, P. (2018). Mortality as framed by ongoingness in digital design. *Design Issues, 34*(1), 95–107. https://doi.org/10.1162/desi_a_00479

Walter, D. (2019). Memento mori: A positive and contemporary reflection through visual art on a life spent well. *IAFOR Journal of Arts & Humanities, 6*(2), 107–120. https://doi.org/10.22492/ijah.6.2.10

Weaver, T. (2019a, September 11). *Stoicism: It's meaning and definition.* Orion Philosophy. https://www.orionphilosophy.com/stoic-blog/stoicism-meaning-and-definition

Weaver, T. (2019b, October 9). *Amor fati & its meaning in Stoicism.* Orion Philosophy. https://www.orionphilosophy.com/stoic-blog/amor-fati-meaning-stoicism

Weaver, T. (2019c, October 10). *Memento mori: How Stoics use death to appreciate life.* Orion Philosophy. https://orionphilosophy.com/memento-mori/

Weaver, T. (2019d, November 4). *Stoicism & the dichotomy of control.* Orion Philosophy. https://www.orionphilosophy.com/stoic-blog/stoicism-and-the-dichotomy-of-control

Weaver, T. (2022a, July 21). *Stoicism and material wealth?* Orion Philosophy. https://orionphilosophy.com/how-do-the-stoics-approach-material-wealth/

Weaver, T. (2022b, August 2). *Stoicism and relationships*. Orion Philosophy. https://orionphilosophy.com/stoicism-and-relationships/

Weaver, T. (2023a, January 11). *What is Stoic eudaimonia?* Orion Philosophy. https://www.orionphilosophy.com/stoic-blog/what-is-stoic-eudaimonia

Weaver, T. (2023b, November 27). *Who is Seneca? Wisdom from the tutor of Rome's most tyrannical emperor*. Orion Philosophy. https://www.orionphilosophy.com/stoic-blog/who-is-seneca

Weaver, T. (2023c, December 19). *How Stoic indifference unlocks resilience*. Orion Philosophy. https://www.orionphilosophy.com/stoic-blog/how-stoic-indifference-unlocks-resilience

Weaver, T. (2023d, December 19). *The Stoic philosophy of Gaius Musonius Rufus*. Orion Philosophy. https://www.orionphilosophy.com/stoic-blog/the-stoic-philosophy-of-gaius-musonius-rufus

Weaver, T. (2023e, December 19). *Who is Zeno of Citium? The father of Stoic philosophy*. Orion Philosophy. https://www.orionphilosophy.com/stoic-blog/zeno-of-citium

Weaver, T. (2024, March 9). *Stoics use the power of death to better appreciate life*. Orion Philosophy. https://orionphilosophy.com/memento-mori/

WebMD Editorial Contributors. (2021, October 25). *Mental health benefits of decluttering*. WebMD. https://www.webmd.com/mental-health/mental-health-benefits-of-decluttering

What is memento mori? A Stoic reflection on life and death (n.d.). Stoic. https://www.getstoic.com/blog/what-is-memento-mori-stoicism

What is Stoicism? (2013, October 22). Modern Stoicism. https://modernstoicism.com/what-is-stoicism/

Whelan, E. (2019, December 6). *Epictetus: Philosophy as a Guide to Life*. Classical Wisdom Weekly. https://classicalwisdom.com/people/philosophers/epictetus-philosophy-as-a-guide-to-life/

Who was Marcus Aurelius? An introduction to the last great emperor, leader and Stoic of Rome. (n.d.). Farnam Street. https://fs.blog/intellectual-giants/marcus-aurelius/

Wooll, M. (2021, July 26). *A growth mindset is a must-have—these 13 tips Will grow yours.* BetterUp. https://www.betterup.com/blog/growth-mindset

Wu, G., Feder, A., Cohen, H., Kim, J. J., Calderon, S., Charney, D. S., & Mathé, A. A. (2013). Understanding resilience. *Frontiers in Behavioral Neuroscience, 7*(10). https://doi.org/10.3389/fnbeh.2013.00010

Yeager, D. S., & Dweck, C. S. (2012). Mindsets that promote resilience: When students believe that personal characteristics can be developed. *Educational Psychologist, 47*(4), 302–314. https://doi.org/10.1080/00461520.2012.722805

Yeung, A. (2020, May 3). *This simple tool will supercharge your courage, motivation, and focus (In just 15 seconds a week).* Anthony J. Yeung. https://www.anthonyjyeung.com/memento-mori-life/